A Neuroscientist Sees What AI Is Becoming

The Mysterious Future of AI

How a Neuroscientist Diagnoses
the Machine Mind

Moawiah Naffaa, PhD

Copyright

First Edition, 2026

Published by
Moawiah Naffaa

For inquiries, permissions, or rights requests, please contact:

Email: Moawiah.Naffaa@proton.me

Cover design: Moawiah Naffaa
Interior illustrations: Moawiah Naffaa

Disclaimer

The terms **Artificial Patient**, **Artificial Cognitive Medicine**, *diagnosis*, *symptom*, *prognosis*, *intervention*, and related clinical language are used in this book as conceptual frameworks for investigating artificial intelligence systems. They do not imply that AI systems are biological organisms, human patients, conscious or sentient beings, or subjects of literal medical diagnosis or treatment.

References to neuroscience identify principles of scientific investigation that may be useful for studying learned artificial systems. They do not suggest that artificial neural networks function biologically like the human brain. The comparison concerns the investigation of development, internal organization, observable behavior, causal intervention, and change over time.

Table of Contents

Preface

I came to artificial intelligence with questions shaped by neuroscience.

In neuroscience, observing what a system does is rarely the end of the investigation. A behavior may be obvious while its mechanism remains uncertain. Activity in a particular region may accompany a function without causing it. Damage to one pathway may produce little visible impairment because another pathway compensates. The same stimulus may generate different responses depending on attention, prior experience, internal state, or context. An intervention may change behavior immediately while leaving the organization that produced the original condition largely intact.

The questions therefore become deeper very quickly.

What process produced the behavior?

Which components were actually necessary?

How did the present organization develop?

What changed when the system moved into another state?

Would the same mechanism operate under different conditions?

If the behavior improved, what inside the system had actually changed?

These are ordinary scientific questions when studying the brain. They arise because cognition is not produced by isolated components acting independently. It emerges from organized interactions among processes whose roles depend on history, context, and the state of the larger system.

When I began thinking more seriously about modern artificial intelligence, I found myself asking the same kinds of questions.

AI was usually presented to me through what it could do. A new model could answer harder questions, generate better code, interpret images, reason across longer contexts, use tools, or perform well on another benchmark. Each advance demonstrated something important. Yet my attention kept moving beneath the result.

I wanted to know what produced those capabilities, whether apparently similar models relied on the same internal processes, whether

Preface

I came to artificial intelligence with questions shaped by neuroscience.

In neuroscience, observing what a system does is rarely the end of the investigation. A behavior may be obvious while its mechanism remains uncertain. Activity in a particular region may accompany a function without causing it. Damage to one pathway may produce little visible impairment because another pathway compensates. The same stimulus may generate different responses depending on attention, prior experience, internal state, or context. An intervention may change behavior immediately while leaving the organization that produced the original condition largely intact.

The questions therefore become deeper very quickly.

What process produced the behavior?

Which components were actually necessary?

How did the present organization develop?

What changed when the system moved into another state?

Would the same mechanism operate under different conditions?

If the behavior improved, what inside the system had actually changed?

These are ordinary scientific questions when studying the brain. They arise because cognition is not produced by isolated components acting independently. It emerges from organized interactions among processes whose roles depend on history, context, and the state of the larger system.

When I began thinking more seriously about modern artificial intelligence, I found myself asking the same kinds of questions.

AI was usually presented to me through what it could do. A new model could answer harder questions, generate better code, interpret images, reason across longer contexts, use tools, or perform well on another benchmark. Each advance demonstrated something important. Yet my attention kept moving beneath the result.

I wanted to know what produced those capabilities, whether apparently similar models relied on the same internal processes, whether

intervention changed a mechanism or only its expression, and whether an explanation remained valid as the system continued to learn.

The more I considered these questions, the less natural it seemed to think of a trained AI system only as finished software.

Training gives the system a history.

Representations emerge and become reorganized. Some strategies strengthen while others weaken. Different pathways may compete. One process may compensate for weakness elsewhere. Later learning acts on an organization already shaped by everything that came before it. The system that exists at the end of training is therefore not explained completely by knowing the architecture with which training began.

That way of thinking felt familiar.

Neuroscience has spent generations confronting systems whose visible behavior can be easier to observe than the organization producing it. Progress required moving beyond description toward mechanism: combining observation with intervention, studying development through time, comparing alternative explanations, and treating variability not merely as noise but as evidence about how a system is organized.

Artificial intelligence now presents its own version of that scientific challenge.

This book grew from the possibility that the habits of reasoning developed for other complex cognitive systems might help us ask better questions about learned artificial ones.

The most important shift was surprisingly simple.

Instead of asking only whether an AI system works, ask what internal process allows it to work.

Instead of treating a failure as its own explanation, ask what mechanisms could have produced the same outward symptom.

Instead of examining only the system that exists now, reconstruct how that organization emerged.

Instead of assuming that successful intervention means successful repair, investigate what organization remains afterward.

And instead of treating the present system as final, ask how its mechanisms may change as learning continues.

Their value will depend on whether they generate better scientific questions, more discriminating experiments, stronger explanations, and predictions that can be tested against learned systems as they develop.

That is ultimately why I wrote this book.

Artificial intelligence is advancing extraordinarily quickly. The natural response is to ask what the next systems will be able to do.

I became increasingly interested in a different question.

As these systems become more capable, will our understanding of them deepen at the same pace?

Capability can advance through engineering alone.

Understanding requires investigation.

And the habits of neuroscience taught me that when intelligence emerges from a complex adaptive system, the most interesting scientific work often begins after the behavior appears.

Introduction

We Built Intelligence Before We Understood It

Artificial intelligence can now write essays, generate computer code, analyze medical information, identify scientific patterns, and engage in conversations that often appear remarkably human. Abilities that seemed extraordinary only a few years ago are rapidly becoming ordinary.

Beneath these achievements lies a scientific paradox.

We have learned how to build increasingly capable artificial intelligence systems without fully understanding the internal organization that emerges as they learn. Researchers can design neural network architectures, assemble training datasets, optimize billions of parameters, and measure performance with remarkable precision. Yet once training is complete, it remains difficult to explain how a model represents knowledge, organizes concepts, combines information, and produces many of its most sophisticated behaviors.

Performance and understanding are not the same.

A model may produce the correct answer while relying on a fragile strategy. Two systems may achieve the same score through fundamentally different internal processes. An intervention may eliminate an unwanted behavior without correcting the mechanism that produced it. These differences become increasingly consequential as AI enters medicine, scientific discovery, engineering, finance, education, and public decision-making.

Mechanistic interpretability has begun to expose parts of this hidden organization. Researchers can identify features, analyze activations, trace limited circuits, and alter internal components to observe how behavior changes. These methods are beginning to open the black box, but observing a component is not the same as understanding the system. A discovered feature does not by itself reveal how it participates in a larger process, how that process emerged during training, or whether it will remain stable when conditions change.

Science advances when description gives way to explanation. Neuroscience did not progress merely by cataloging neurons, nor biology by listing the parts of living organisms. Understanding required relationships, mechanisms, histories, perturbations, and trajectories.

Artificial intelligence is approaching a similar threshold.

Computer science has taught us how to build and optimize these systems. Interpretability is beginning to reveal aspects of their internal organization. The next challenge is to connect those observations into a richer science of artificial cognition—one capable of asking not only what a system does, but how its internal organization developed, why a particular behavior emerged, how that organization may change, and whether an intervention corrected the underlying mechanism or merely concealed its expression.

These questions will shape how advanced AI systems are evaluated and improved, both before and after deployment. External performance alone cannot reveal whether a model is robust, whether its success depends on unstable shortcuts, whether a failure is likely to recur, or whether two apparently similar systems carry different future risks.

The first era of artificial intelligence was defined by the effort to build machines capable of intelligent behavior.

The next may be defined by a harder task:

Now that we have built intelligence, how do we learn to understand it?

PART I

The Intelligence We Built—but Do Not Yet Fully Understand

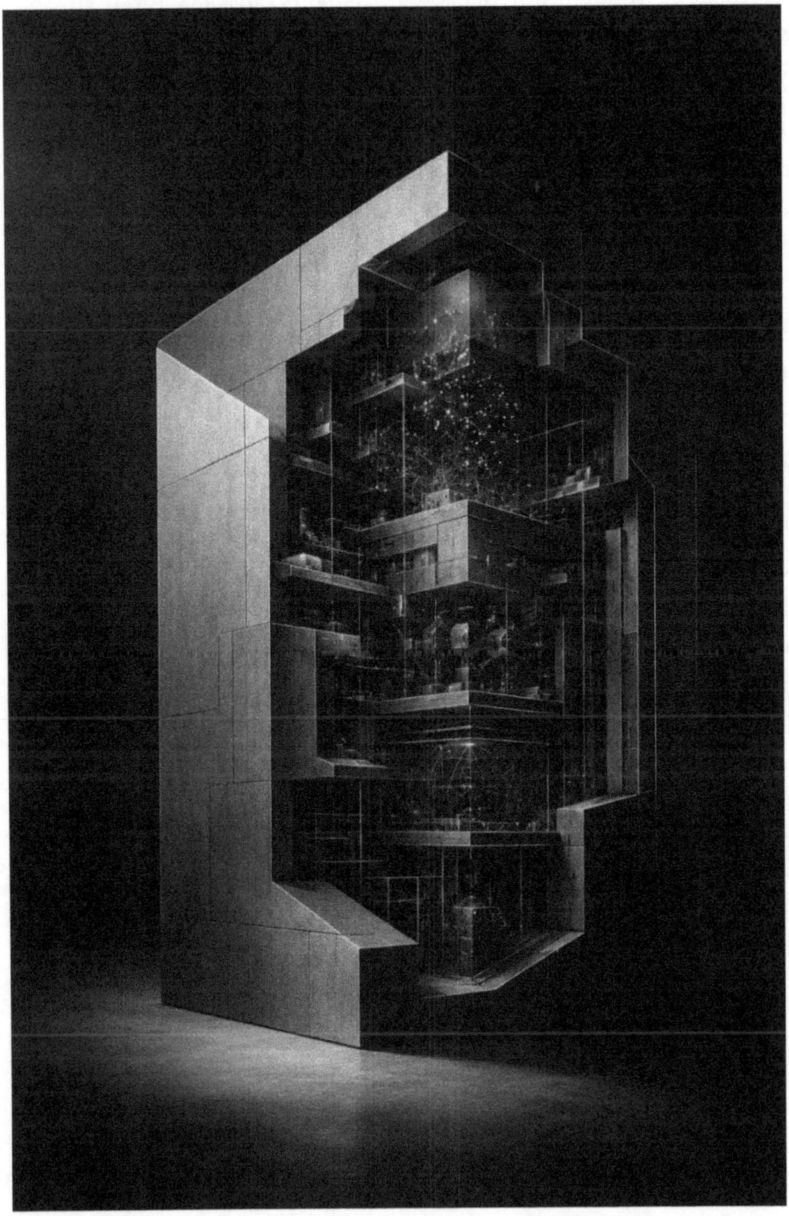

What began as an engineering project soon created a different kind of challenge.

Artificial intelligence systems became increasingly capable of recognizing patterns, generating language, writing code, analyzing images, and solving problems across domains that once required separate programs and carefully specified rules.

The systems became easier to evaluate than to explain.

Researchers can measure what a model accomplishes, but the internal organization responsible for that accomplishment is often less transparent. Training produces representations, associations, and computational pathways that were not individually specified by the engineers who designed the system.

The problem begins with a paradox: a technology deliberately constructed but only partially understood. It deepens as learned systems depart from traditional software, as their internal operations become accessible to investigation, and as the limits of performance-based evaluation become clearer.

The chapters that follow move from construction to learning, from external behavior to internal observation, and from successful performance to the question of what that performance can actually establish.

What kind of understanding is required when capability can be measured more easily than it can be explained?

CHAPTER 1

The Greatest Technological Mystery of Our Time

For most of scientific history, humanity encountered the phenomenon first and the explanation later. People watched the planets move long before they understood gravity. Physicians recognized patterns of disease centuries before microbes became visible. Farmers altered plants and animals through selective breeding long before genetics explained how traits passed from one generation to the next.

Artificial intelligence presents a stranger sequence.

We did not discover it in nature. We built it. Researchers designed the architectures, selected the training methods, assembled the data, and supplied the computational power. Yet the **internal organization** produced through that process remains only partially understood.[1]

None of this is mysterious in the supernatural sense. The mathematics are well established.

The mystery begins only after **learning**.

At the beginning of training, a modern artificial intelligence system contains enormous numbers of adjustable numerical values. Those values do not yet represent recognizable concepts, linguistic rules, scientific relationships, or strategies for solving problems. Through repeated exposure to data, they are modified again and again. Some relationships strengthen, others weaken, and the system gradually becomes capable of producing structured and increasingly flexible behavior.

No engineer writes these capabilities into the model one rule at a time.

The system acquires them through **experience**.

Within its vast network of parameters, information becomes arranged in ways that support prediction, classification, language, reasoning, and problem solving. But this learned organization does not appear as a readable set of instructions. It exists as distributed patterns across layers, connections, and moment-to-moment activations whose collective operation can be far more difficult to explain than the training procedure that produced them.

The phrase *understanding how AI works* therefore conceals two different kinds of knowledge.

The first is **engineering knowledge**.[2]

Engineering knowledge tells us how to construct the system. It describes the architecture, the learning objective, the optimization process, the data pipeline, and the computational machinery required for training. It allows researchers to build larger models, train them more efficiently, and extend their capabilities.

The second is **scientific understanding**.

Scientific understanding begins with the functional patterns that emerge after training. It asks how knowledge is represented, how concepts become related, how information moves through the network, why a particular response is produced, and why some capabilities remain stable while others prove fragile.

A city makes the difference easier to see.

Imagine possessing the complete construction records for a large city. You know where every building stands, which materials were used, how the roads were laid, where electrical cables run, and how water moves through the underground system. You could describe the physical construction of the city in extraordinary detail.

Yet those records would not tell you how the city lives.

They would not explain why one neighborhood becomes a center of commerce while another becomes culturally influential. They would not reveal how traffic patterns shift when thousands of people alter their routines, why particular public spaces attract communities, or how countless local choices combine into the behavior of the city as a whole.

The blueprints describe **construction**. They do not fully explain **organization**.

Modern artificial intelligence poses a comparable problem. Researchers may understand the components from which a model was built while still lacking a complete account of the functional organization that arose during training. The architecture establishes a space of possibilities. The learning process determines which possibilities become embedded in the trained system.

Traditional software rarely created such a wide separation between construction and later behavior.[3]

For decades, computer programs were built through explicit instructions. A programmer defined the rules, wrote the decision logic, and specified how the software should respond under particular conditions. Even highly complicated programs could, at least in principle, be traced back to instructions intentionally placed there by human beings.

When conventional software failed, developers searched for the faulty line, incorrect condition, or missing rule. Its behavior ultimately reflected the logic written into it.

Machine learning changes the source of that logic.

Instead of specifying every rule directly, engineers create a system capable of adjusting itself in response to data. They determine the architecture and the process of learning, but they do not individually specify every solution the model will eventually discover. The detailed configuration is produced through training.

A traditional program resembles an instruction manual. Its logic is explicitly written, even when that manual contains millions of instructions.

A trained neural network is closer to a system that **develops**. Its initial architecture is designed, but its mature form is shaped through experience.

This does not mean artificial intelligence is alive, nor that it learns exactly as a biological organism does. The comparison concerns the relationship between initial design and later organization. In both cases, the starting conditions do not by themselves reveal every pattern that experience will produce.

Consider how a child acquires language.[4]

A child is not born with a written inventory of every word, grammatical construction, metaphor, and social convention that will later become available in speech. Biology supplies a nervous system capable of learning. Experience shapes that system over time.

Neuroscientists can describe many of the mechanisms that make this possible. They can study neurons, synapses, sensory systems, developmental plasticity, and the brain regions involved in language. But those mechanisms alone do not reveal the complete linguistic system that will emerge within one particular child.

The details depend on **developmental history**: the language spoken at home, the sounds repeatedly heard, the people encountered, the stories told, the mistakes corrected, and the associations formed across years of experience.

The architecture makes learning possible. Experience determines what is learned.

Artificial intelligence follows a very different biological and computational path, but a similar explanatory problem appears. The source code describes the machinery of learning. It does not provide a direct map of the knowledge, strategies, and associations created during training.

Inspecting the code of an AI system cannot therefore settle the question of how the trained system produces its behavior.

The code may show how information enters the model, how mathematical operations are performed, how errors are calculated, and how parameters are updated. It may describe the training procedure with complete precision. Yet after billions of updates, the resulting configuration can support internal patterns that were never explicitly named by the engineers who designed it.

A model may learn to distinguish formal from informal language, connect concepts across distant contexts, identify hidden regularities in data, or adopt shortcuts that happen to succeed during testing. These strategies are not stored as neatly labeled rules. They are distributed throughout the network.

That uncertainty becomes especially important when performance appears successful.

Two models can produce the same answer while relying on different internal strategies. One may identify a meaningful relationship in the data. Another may exploit a superficial pattern that disappears as soon as the conditions change. Their outputs may look identical until they encounter a problem that falls outside the familiar pattern.

A correct response may therefore reflect a robust principle, a memorized association, or a shortcut that succeeds only under familiar conditions.

As long as software consisted mainly of rules written by programmers, inspecting those rules provided a plausible path toward explanation. Once systems began learning their own internal solutions, that path was no longer enough.

The central question changed with it.

The problem was no longer simply what instructions had been written into the machine.

It was what learning had placed there instead.

The difficulty is that what learning places inside a model is not arranged for **human inspection**.

A trained artificial intelligence system does not contain a small library of clearly labeled concepts waiting to be opened. There is no single location marked grammar, another marked causality, and another marked scientific reasoning. What the model has learned is distributed across vast numbers of numerical relationships that interact differently depending on the input, the surrounding context, and the activity of the rest of the network.

A concept may not exist in one place at all. It may emerge only when many regions of the system become active together. One pattern may contribute to several capabilities, while a single capability may depend on activity spread throughout the network. Understanding therefore requires more than locating individual components. It requires understanding how those components work together.

Like the music produced by an orchestra, a model's behavior emerges from coordinated contributions whose meaning depends on their relationships across time.[5]

Neuroscience confronted a similar challenge. Early investigators often searched for individual brain regions responsible for complete mental functions. Some forms of specialization proved real, but the broader picture became increasingly clear: memory, language, attention, and reasoning emerge through **interacting networks** rather than isolated locations.

Identifying an active region is not the same as explaining the process in which it participates. Likewise, identifying an internal feature within an AI system is not the same as understanding the capability it supports.

Researchers can inspect individual artificial neurons, record patterns of activation, alter selected connections, or follow information through successive layers. Each observation provides evidence. None, in isolation, supplies a complete explanation.

The model's organization is therefore not merely hidden. It is **relational**.

Learning makes the problem harder because it alters the whole network rather than adding one independent skill at a time. Every new pattern is incorporated into a system that already contains countless other relationships. Training can strengthen one pathway, weaken another, reshape existing associations, or change how previously acquired information is used.

The behavior of the finished model reflects not only its latest experience but the entire **history of learning** that produced it.

As a result, two models built from the same architecture may develop different internal solutions.

They may be trained with the same objective, exposed to similar data, and achieve nearly identical performance on standard evaluations. Yet one model may arrange knowledge around relationships that continue to work when conditions change, while another may depend on regularities that merely resemble its training experience.

The difference becomes visible only when the environment changes.

Consider a medical student learning to interpret an electrocardiogram. One student understands how electrical activity moves through the heart and how disturbances in conduction alter the waveform. Another has memorized the appearance of common abnormalities. During a routine examination, both may reach the same diagnosis.

Present an unfamiliar tracing or combine two uncommon abnormalities, however, and the difference quickly appears. The visible answer had concealed two different forms of **understanding**.

Small changes in wording, context, or task structure can expose whether the earlier success depended on a transferable relationship or a narrow regularity.

Performance that once appeared stable may suddenly fracture.

The **failure** itself becomes informative.

It is no longer merely evidence that the model produced a wrong answer. It becomes evidence about the internal process that produced the earlier success. A dependence on superficial cues, an unstable representation, or a fragile reasoning strategy may remain invisible until familiar conditions disappear.

Errors can also reveal where a process broke down. A model may lack the relevant information, possess it but fail to retrieve it, or activate competing patterns that interfere with the correct response. The outward result may look similar even when the underlying cause is different.

The same caution applies to apparent improvement.

Suppose a model repeatedly produces an undesirable response and researchers modify it until that response disappears. From the outside, the intervention appears successful. Yet the underlying tendency may have been reorganized, weakened, redirected, or merely made more difficult to trigger.

The disappearance of a behavior does not automatically reveal what changed inside the system.

Behavior is evidence, but it is not a complete explanation.

Performance tells us what a model did under particular conditions. Scientific understanding asks how that behavior was produced, what representations and interactions supported it, and whether they will remain reliable when the conditions change.

The challenge is no longer simply to measure increasingly capable artificial intelligence systems. It is to explain the learned mechanisms beneath their behavior.

Science repeatedly reaches moments when describing a phenomenon is no longer enough. Progress depends on discovering the **mechanisms** that produce it.

Artificial intelligence has reached such a threshold.

Its systems can now write, translate, program, create images, analyze information, and solve increasingly complex problems. Yet their expanding capabilities have made the unanswered questions beneath those capabilities more consequential.

How is knowledge represented across a learned network? How do distributed patterns combine to produce a conclusion? Why do some capabilities survive changes in context while others collapse? What distinguishes genuine generalization from a familiar pattern successfully repeated?

These are no longer secondary questions. As artificial intelligence moves beyond controlled evaluations and into changing, uncertain, and unfamiliar environments, its reliability will depend on more than whether it can produce a correct response. It will depend on the learned organization that produces that response and on whether that organization remains stable when familiar conditions disappear.

The chapters that follow examine that hidden organization, the sources of stability and fragility within it, and the scientific methods needed to distinguish robust understanding from performance that only appears dependable.

Artificial intelligence is no longer only a technology to be built and measured. It has become a complex learned system whose internal organization must be investigated if its capabilities, limitations, and future development are to be understood.

ENDNOTES

1. Modern deep neural networks are engineered using well-established architectures, optimization algorithms, and training procedures. However, many of the internal representations and computational strategies that emerge during learning remain only partially understood. This distinction has motivated the rapidly growing field of mechanistic interpretability.

2. The distinction developed in this chapter between engineering knowledge (how a system is constructed) and scientific understanding (how a learned system functions internally after training) represents the central conceptual framework proposed throughout this book.

3. Conventional software engineering relies primarily on explicitly programmed logic. Modern machine-learning systems instead acquire much of their effective computational organization during optimization over data, making their learned internal organization an additional scientific object of investigation.

4. The comparison with language development is illustrative rather than biological. It highlights the distinction between an initial architecture and experience-dependent organization. It does not suggest that artificial neural networks learn through the same biological mechanisms as the human brain.

5. The orchestra analogy is an original explanatory analogy introduced by the author to illustrate how coordinated interactions among many components can produce functions that are not attributable to any single component in isolation.

CHAPTER 2

Why AI Is Different from Traditional Software

For most of the history of computing, software behaved according to instructions written directly by human beings.

A programmer defined the possible inputs, established the rules that connected those inputs to particular operations, and specified what the system should produce. The program could be complicated, but its logic remained explicit. Its behavior arose from instructions deliberately placed within it.

A tax program might contain rules for calculating deductions. A navigation system might compare routes using predefined criteria. A chess program might search through possible moves using procedures selected by its designers. Each system could process enormous amounts of information, but the relationship between its construction and its behavior remained comparatively direct.

The program did what its instructions told it to do.

Machine learning altered that relationship.

Instead of writing every rule required to solve a problem, engineers began constructing systems that could discover useful patterns through training. The programmer no longer needed to specify every feature that distinguished one object from another, every grammatical relationship that gave a sentence meaning, or every sequence of steps required to produce a successful answer.

The system could learn those relationships from data.

This shift did not eliminate programming. It changed what programming was used to create.

The engineer still defines the broad machinery. The architecture determines how information can enter the model, how signals can move through it, which quantities can be adjusted, and how success or failure is measured during training. The learning algorithm determines how errors alter the model. The training data determines what examples the model encounters.

But the detailed solution is not written directly.

It is produced through **optimization**.[1]

Suppose a programmer wants a computer to distinguish cats from dogs.

One approach would be to define a long list of visible features. Cats may have particular facial proportions, ear shapes, body sizes, or movement patterns. Dogs may differ along those dimensions. The program could measure those features and apply a decision rule.

But such rules quickly become fragile.

A cat may be photographed from an unusual angle. Its ears may be hidden. A dog may resemble a cat in size or facial structure. Lighting, background, motion, breed, age, and camera quality may alter every feature the programmer attempted to define.

A machine-learning system approaches the problem differently.

It receives many examples labeled as cats or dogs. During training, it adjusts its internal parameters so that its predictions become more accurate. No single rule tells it what a cat is. Instead, patterns useful for the distinction become distributed across the network.

Some parts of the system may respond to edges or textures. Others may become sensitive to shapes, spatial arrangements, or combinations of features. Deeper layers may integrate these signals into increasingly abstract representations.

The final judgment emerges from their interaction.

The resulting definition emerged through training rather than from a written rule.

That definition is not stored as a sentence.

It is not contained in one parameter.

It exists across the network.

A programmer can inspect a conventional instruction such as:

If the temperature falls below a defined threshold, activate the heating system.

The rule is explicit. Its meaning can be read directly. If the heating system activates at the wrong temperature, the condition can be located and corrected.

A neural network does not usually contain an equivalent statement written in human-readable form. Its response depends on the combined activity of many units, each influenced by numerous weighted connections. The meaning of an individual component depends on the larger configuration in which it participates.

Explicit programs work well when the relevant rules are known and can be stated clearly. They are effective in environments where inputs, conditions, and desired outputs can be defined in advance.

Many forms of intelligence do not fit that description.

Language contains ambiguities, implied meanings, shifting contexts, and patterns too numerous to list individually. Visual recognition must remain stable across changes in position, lighting, scale, background, and perspective. Scientific reasoning may require connecting ideas that were never presented together in exactly the same form.

Writing a complete rulebook for such tasks is extremely difficult.

Learning allows the system to extract regularities from examples rather than waiting for a programmer to describe every one of them.

Competence now arises from relationships shaped during training rather than from a procedure fully specified in advance.

A learned model can sometimes respond to unfamiliar situations by using similarities between a new input and patterns encountered during training. It can combine information, extend associations, and apply learned relationships to examples that were never presented in exactly the same form.

This ability is called **generalization**.[2]

Generalization allows a system to move beyond memorizing individual examples. But it is not guaranteed.

A model may learn a relationship that reflects the true organization of a problem. It may also learn a shortcut that happens to work within the training data.

Imagine a system trained to identify a particular animal in photographs. If most images of that animal contain snow in the background, the model may use the snowy environment as a predictive clue. Its performance may appear excellent until the animal appears in a forest.

The system did learn.[3]

It simply learned the wrong relationship.

Training does not transfer human intentions directly into the model. It rewards whichever internal strategy improves performance under the conditions provided.

The optimization process does not ask whether the model's solution matches the explanation a human would prefer. It adjusts parameters in the direction that reduces error.

If a superficial pattern predicts the answer, the model may use it.

If a deeper relationship predicts the answer, the model may use that instead.

The objective determines what counts as success. It does not fully determine how success will be achieved.

Engineers may believe they are training a system to recognize disease in medical images. The model may instead become sensitive to differences in scanners, hospital markings, image formats, or patterns associated with where the data were collected.

The output may still be correct during testing.

The internal basis of that correctness may be unreliable.

Traditional software can also contain hidden assumptions and unintended interactions. Complex programs may behave in surprising ways, but the relevant logic was generally written as code, even if tracing it became difficult.

A learned model reflects more than its architecture. It carries the accumulated effects of the data it encountered, the order and frequency of those examples, the objective used during training, the corrections applied during fine-tuning, and the feedback used to reinforce preferred behavior.

Its history becomes part of its functional organization.[4]

This changes the nature of debugging.

In conventional software, two copies of the same program running under the same conditions are expected to follow the same instructions. When one produces an error, the investigation begins with the code, the input, or the state of the system.

A trained model presents a different problem.

A bug report can identify an undesirable output without revealing which learned process produced it. Debugging must therefore investigate the trained organization rather than search only for an explicitly written faulty instruction.

The difficulty is not simply that the model contains many parameters. It is that those parameters participate in overlapping learned relationships.

Learning does not usually add one independent function at a time.

When a programmer adds a feature to a conventional application, the new instructions can often be separated from the rest of the program. A new button triggers a new routine. A new rule modifies a defined decision path.

New training changes a network that already contains many existing relationships.

An update intended to strengthen one capability may alter another. Fine-tuning may improve performance in one domain while weakening it elsewhere. New knowledge may compete with older patterns or become entangled with them.

The model changes as a system.

A language model does not necessarily possess one isolated mechanism for grammar, another for factual knowledge, and another for reasoning. These functions may depend on overlapping representations and shared computational pathways.[5]

The same internal features may contribute to several behaviors.

Changing those features may therefore produce consequences beyond the behavior being targeted. Correcting an output does not always isolate the underlying cause, and altering one learned pattern may affect others that depend on the same internal resources.

The difficulty cannot be explained by size alone.

Modern models may contain billions of adjustable parameters and process information through many layers. Scale increases the difficulty of inspection, but size alone does not explain why learned systems are hard to interpret.

A very large conventional database may contain billions of entries and still remain conceptually straightforward. Each entry has a defined location and meaning. Complexity increases the effort required to search it, but not necessarily the nature of the explanation.

A learned network is different because its internal elements gain meaning through interaction.

The relevant unit may not be an individual parameter or artificial neuron. It may be a pattern distributed across many components. That pattern may appear only for certain inputs, disappear in others, and combine with different patterns depending on context.

The model's internal activity is dynamic.

A word does not always produce the same effect. Its role depends on the sentence around it, the information that came before it, and the relationships activated elsewhere in the network.

The same internal component may participate in different processes at different times.

Interpretation must therefore address both **representation** and **computation**.

Representation concerns what information has been encoded within the system.

Computation concerns how that information is transformed and used to produce an output.

A model may contain relevant knowledge but fail to retrieve it. It may retrieve several competing possibilities and select the wrong one. It may represent a concept accurately in one context but distort it when other signals interfere.

The final response alone does not reveal which process occurred.

Traditional software invites a question such as:

Which instruction produced this output?

A learned model often requires a different set of questions:

Which representations became active?

How did they interact?

Which pathways carried the information?

What alternatives competed with the selected response?

Which parts of the process were stable, and which depended on the immediate context?

Artificial intelligence is still software. It runs on hardware, executes mathematical operations, and follows computational procedures. But the functional organization responsible for its advanced behavior emerges through training.

That difference changes how failure must be investigated.

It changes how reliability must be evaluated.

It changes what it means to understand the system.

The central object is no longer only the code that makes learning possible. It is the **learned model** that training produced.

That model contains the accumulated consequences of data, optimization, feedback, and experience. Its abilities cannot be reduced to the architecture alone, just as the behavior of a conventional program cannot be explained by examining the computer on which it runs.

The architecture provides the machinery.

Learning creates the internal organization through which the machinery becomes capable.

Traditional software showed that human beings could translate rules into machines.

Machine learning showed that machines could develop useful internal solutions without those solutions being written in advance.

That achievement created a new scientific problem.[6]

The code explains how the system was allowed to learn.

It does not, by itself, explain what the system became.

ENDNOTES

1. Optimization refers to the iterative adjustment of model parameters using objective functions that reduce prediction error during training. The resulting computational organization emerges through learning rather than explicit programming.

2. Generalization describes the ability of a learned model to perform appropriately on new examples that were not encountered during training. Understanding how and why models generalize remains an active area of artificial intelligence research.

3. Machine-learning systems may acquire predictive strategies that exploit statistical regularities without capturing the underlying structure of a problem. Such shortcut learning has become an important topic in research on robustness and generalization.

4. A trained model reflects the cumulative effects of its developmental history, including data exposure, optimization, fine-tuning, reinforcement, and later adaptation. Earlier learning can influence how later information is represented and processed.

5. Modern neural networks frequently represent information through distributed and overlapping internal representations rather than isolated symbolic locations. A single internal feature may contribute to multiple behaviors, while a single behavior may depend on many interacting representations.

6. The interpretation developed in this chapter—that learned artificial systems require scientific investigation beyond engineering description—represents the conceptual framework proposed throughout this book rather than an established classification within the artificial intelligence literature.

CHAPTER 3

Looking Inside the Machine

Imagine encountering an unfamiliar animal capable of navigating obstacles, recognizing individuals, remembering locations, and adjusting its behavior when circumstances change.

You could observe what it does.

You could record when it succeeds, identify the conditions under which it fails, and compare its performance with that of other animals. Over time, you might develop an increasingly accurate description of its abilities.

But behavior alone would leave crucial questions unanswered.

How does it recognize a familiar face? Where is a recent experience retained? Which internal processes guide a decision? Does a successful response depend on a stable representation of the environment, or on a shortcut that happens to work under familiar conditions?

Eventually, observation from the outside reaches its limit.

To explain the behavior, researchers must investigate the system producing it.

Artificial intelligence has reached that point.

External evaluation reveals what a system can accomplish. Mechanistic interpretability begins where that evidence stops: with the internal representations, pathways, and transformations that produced the result.

Researchers have therefore begun investigating trained models from the inside.

This effort has given rise to **mechanistic interpretability**, a field that seeks to connect internal activity with the computations and behaviors produced by a model.[1]

Instead of asking only whether the model generated the correct answer, researchers ask:

What information was represented?

Which components became active?

How did those components interact?

Where did information move?

Which internal changes would alter the result?

The emphasis shifts from evaluating performance to reconstructing process.

The architecture, learning algorithm, and objective function define the conditions under which a model learns. They do not provide a direct account of the internal configuration produced by training.

Developmental biology offers a useful comparison.

A genome contains instructions essential to building an organism. Yet reading its DNA sequence does not reveal the complete arrangement of the mature body. Development emerges through interactions among genes, cells, chemical signals, environmental conditions, and the sequence of events through which tissues form.

The resulting organism cannot be understood from its initial instructions alone.

A trained model presents a related explanatory problem.

Training transforms an initial computational framework into a functioning system containing representations, pathways, and regularities that cannot be read directly from its design.

Researchers must therefore study the **trained system itself**.

Training a neural network and investigating the network after training have become distinct scientific activities.

One produces a capable model.

The other attempts to determine how that capability is arranged internally.

Mechanistic interpretability provides methods for carrying out that investigation. Researchers can record patterns of internal activity, compare representations, trace the movement of information, alter selected components, and examine how those interventions affect behavior.

The trained model no longer has to be treated as one indivisible computational object.

Its internal operations can be divided into smaller questions that can be observed and tested.

3.1 Features Within the Network

One of the first challenges is determining what meaningful internal activity looks like.

A neural network contains enormous numbers of numerical activations. Most of these values are not immediately interpretable. A raw activation does not arrive with a label identifying it as grammar, geography, uncertainty, code, or biological knowledge.

Researchers search instead for recurring patterns that correspond reliably to properties of the information being processed.

These patterns are often called **features**.[2]

A feature is not a word stored inside the model.

It is not a complete memory or an isolated idea.

It is a pattern of internal activity that responds to some recurring property of an input or computation.

Some features respond strongly to punctuation or quotation marks. Others become active for programming syntax, chemical structures, biological terminology, foreign languages, geographical locations, mathematical expressions, or particular semantic relationships.

Some are concrete.

Others are highly abstract.

A feature may respond not merely to a particular word but to a category, relationship, style, or functional role shared across many different examples.

These patterns were not individually written by engineers. They emerged because the model needed useful internal distinctions in order to perform its training task.

The discovery of features also changed the level at which researchers searched for meaning.

Early attempts to understand neural networks often focused on individual artificial neurons. Researchers hoped that a single neuron might correspond neatly to one recognizable concept.

Occasionally, individual neurons do show strong and interpretable selectivity.

But the general picture is more complicated.

A single neuron may contribute to multiple processes. The same neuron may respond during programming tasks, mathematical expressions, foreign-language text, and biological discussions, depending on the surrounding context.

Likewise, one concept may depend on coordinated activity distributed across many neurons.[3]

The meaningful object is often not the individual neuron but the **feature represented through a pattern of activity**.

The question therefore changes from:

Which neuron stores this concept?

to:

Which internal pattern consistently represents it?

This shift resembles a central lesson from neuroscience: complex functions rarely belong to isolated cells. They arise through coordinated activity among interacting populations.

Within artificial networks, meaning likewise often depends on patterns rather than single locations.

Identifying a feature, however, does not reveal how it participates in a computation.

Researchers must also determine when it becomes active.

3.2 Activations in Context

Whenever a model processes information, its internal components respond to different degrees.

Some become strongly active.

Others contribute weakly.

Many remain largely inactive.

The pattern changes as new information enters the model and as the computation progresses.

An **activation** reflects the participation of a component at a particular moment.

By recording activations, researchers can examine how the model responds internally to different words, images, prompts, or tasks.

A feature associated with a broad topic may appear early as the model identifies what a passage concerns. Other activity may emerge when grammatical relationships are established, when a factual association is retrieved, or when a mathematical operation is performed.

The sequence matters.

A model generating an answer does not activate every relevant representation simultaneously. Information is selected, transformed, combined, and redirected across successive stages of computation.

Activation analysis makes portions of that process visible.[4]

A single activation pattern, however, is like one frame from a film.

It captures a moment.

It does not reveal the full sequence that produced the outcome.

Researchers therefore examine how groups of internal components cooperate over time.

3.3 Circuits and Information Flow

A **circuit** is a functional pathway through which information contributes to a computation.[5]

It is not a physical wire inside the model.

It is a pattern of coordinated activity connecting multiple components whose interaction performs a recognizable operation.

One feature may identify relevant information.

Another may transform it.

A third may compare it with context.

A later component may influence which possible output receives the greatest support.

No single component performs the entire computation. The result arises from the sequence and interaction among them.

Circuits shift attention from isolated activity to coordinated information flow.

Researchers ask:

Which features interacted?

In what order?

Which pathways carried the information?

Where was the information transformed?

Which stage influenced the final answer?

These questions have revealed compact computational structures within some neural networks.

Researchers have traced circuits involved in tasks such as recognizing repeated patterns, connecting pronouns with earlier nouns, identifying indirect objects, or moving information from one position in a sequence to another.[6]

Such findings show that trained models can develop recurring computational arrangements rather than relying on completely unstructured activity.

But circuits are not always cleanly separated.

The same components may support different operations under different conditions. A pathway important for one task may share resources with others. The boundaries between computations may shift according to context.

The model is therefore not a collection of independent miniature programs.

Its internal operations intersect.

3.4 Superposition and Sparse Representations

That intersection creates one of interpretability's central difficulties.

Individual neurons often respond to several seemingly unrelated properties.

A neuron may contribute to code, mathematics, biological terminology, and a foreign language at different moments. Its activity may appear to combine independent features within the same representational space.

This phenomenon is known as **superposition**.[7]

Superposition allows a model to represent more features than it has individual dimensions available to assign separately. Multiple signals are encoded through shared combinations of activity.

This is efficient for the model.

It is difficult for the researcher.

If many concepts contribute to the activity of the same neurons, inspecting those neurons individually may produce a confusing mixture rather than a clean explanation.

Researchers therefore attempt to separate the combined signals into more interpretable components.

One promising approach involves **sparse representations**.[8]

Sparse methods seek a set of underlying features in which only a relatively small number are strongly active at any moment. The objective is to recover representations that correspond more clearly to recognizable concepts or computational functions.

The process resembles separating several musical instruments recorded onto one audio track.

The original recording contains every instrument at once. Their sounds blend together, making individual contributions difficult to isolate.

Signal separation attempts to recover the distinct instruments from the combined recording.

Sparse representations pursue a related goal within a neural network. Rather than treating individual neurons as the fundamental units of meaning, they search for latent features whose combinations produced the observed neuronal activity.

This approach has revealed internal features associated with a wide range of linguistic, conceptual, technical, and behavioral patterns.

Some features are immediately understandable.

Others resist simple description.

A feature may respond to a combination of properties that has no obvious label in ordinary language. Another may contribute to distinct processes whose relationship is not apparent to the researcher.

The internal configuration of a model was shaped for successful computation, not for human readability.

Interpretability must therefore reconstruct a system whose categories may not align neatly with human concepts.

The resulting picture is partial but increasingly detailed.

Researchers can identify recurring features, examine when they become active, and trace some of the circuits through which they participate in computation.

The next step is to determine whether these structures merely correlate with behavior or actually help produce it.

3.5 From Observation to Intervention

Suppose a feature consistently becomes active whenever a model reasons about geographical locations.

The association is suggestive.

It is not yet causal.

The feature may contribute directly to geographical reasoning. It may respond to the result of a process occurring elsewhere. It may be activated by a related contextual signal without playing any necessary role in the computation.

Researchers distinguish among these possibilities by intervening.

They may suppress the feature while the model performs a geographical task. If the model begins making geographical errors while unrelated abilities remain largely intact, the evidence for a causal contribution becomes stronger.

Researchers may also increase the feature's activity. If the model begins introducing geographical concepts into otherwise unrelated contexts, the intervention provides further information about its function.

The question is no longer merely:

What became active?

It becomes:

What changes when that activity is altered?

This experimental logic allows researchers to move from correlations toward causal accounts of internal computation.[9]

This progression from observation to causal explanation is summarized in **Figure 1.**

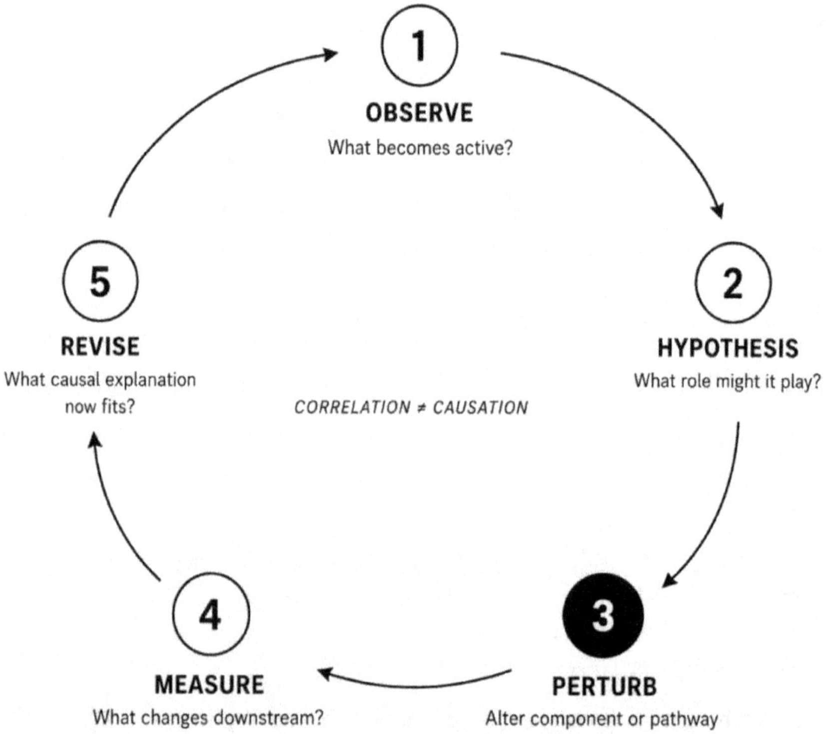

Figure 1. From Observation to Causal Explanation.

3.6 Activation Patching

One influential method is **activation patching**.[10]

Imagine two closely matched inputs.

With one input, the model produces the correct answer.

With the other, it fails.

Researchers record the internal activity generated during both computations. They then replace the activity at one selected location in the unsuccessful run with the corresponding activity from the successful run.

Everything else remains unchanged.

If the model's answer becomes correct, the patched activity likely contributed to the successful computation.

By repeating this process at different locations and stages, researchers can determine where information relevant to the answer entered the computation, how it moved, and which internal transformations mattered.

Activation patching does not simply ask where information is represented.

It asks where a difference in internal processing changes the outcome.

The method is especially useful when two inputs differ in only one critical respect. Researchers can compare the resulting computations and identify where the model's internal processing begins to diverge.

A complex behavioral difference can then be narrowed to a smaller set of candidate mechanisms.

3.7 Ablation

A related approach is **ablation.**[11]

Instead of replacing internal activity, researchers disable or remove selected components and observe the consequences.

If suppressing a pathway consistently prevents the model from completing a particular task, that pathway likely contributes to the computation.

If performance remains unchanged, several interpretations are possible. The component may be unrelated to the task. Another pathway may compensate for its loss. The model may contain redundant mechanisms capable of producing the same result.

Absence becomes informative.

Failure becomes evidence.

Ablation can reveal which components are necessary under particular conditions, but necessity may depend on context. A pathway essential for one type of prompt may be replaceable in another. A component may become important only when a competing pathway is unavailable.

The experiment therefore identifies causal dependence within a defined situation rather than a permanent, context-free role.

The comparison with neuroscience is methodological, not biological: trained neural networks are not brains, and artificial neurons are not biological neurons. Both fields nevertheless use perturbation to distinguish active participation from passive correlation.

3.8 Model Editing

Researchers can also modify a model's internal representations more directly.

Suppose a model repeatedly associates a historical event with the wrong year.

Retraining the entire system may be unnecessary. Researchers may instead identify internal parameters or representations associated with the incorrect information and alter them selectively.

This process is known as **model editing**.[12]

A successful edit changes the targeted behavior while preserving unrelated capabilities.

If correcting one internal representation reliably changes future answers, that result provides evidence about where and how the information contributed to the model's behavior.

But edits often reveal that knowledge is not neatly isolated.

A change intended to correct one fact may influence related facts, linguistic patterns, or reasoning processes. The edited representation may serve multiple functions. Other parts of the network may reintroduce the original response under a different prompt.

These outcomes are scientifically useful even when the edit is imperfect.

They expose dependencies that passive observation might not reveal.

An intervention becomes a probe of internal arrangement.

The model discloses aspects of its internal structure through the pattern of changes that follows.

3.9 Representation and Computation

The distinction between **representation** and **computation** becomes central.

Representation concerns what information is encoded within the model.

Computation concerns how that information is transformed and used.

A model may possess an accurate representation of a scientific principle but fail to apply it during reasoning.

It may retrieve relevant information yet combine it with an inappropriate contextual pattern.

It may activate several competing representations and select the wrong one.

It may represent a fact correctly in one context but fail to access it when the prompt changes.

A wrong answer therefore does not reveal whether the model lacked the information, failed to retrieve it, transformed it incorrectly, or allowed another process to override it.

Two models may contain similar representations while using them differently.

Conversely, similar computations may operate on differently configured representations.

A complete account requires both.

Researchers therefore ask not only:

What does the model know?

but also:

How is that knowledge transformed into behavior?

This distinction moves interpretability beyond locating internal content.

The object of investigation becomes the coordinated computation unfolding across the network.

3.10 The Limits of Visibility

Mechanistic interpretability has made many previously inaccessible processes observable.

Researchers can identify features, examine activation patterns, reconstruct circuits, separate combined representations, patch internal activity, remove selected components, and alter stored associations.

The hidden system has become more visible.

Visibility is not yet a complete explanation.

A microscope may reveal the shape and internal structures of a cell. Those observations become scientifically meaningful only when they are connected to metabolism, signaling, reproduction, development, and interaction with the surrounding tissue.

Likewise, an interpretable feature gains meaning through the larger process in which it participates.

A circuit may contribute to factual retrieval without explaining how the relevant knowledge was acquired. An activation pattern may predict a response without explaining why that pattern becomes stable in one context and fragile in another. A successful intervention may establish causal participation without revealing how the affected mechanism interacts with the rest of the model across thousands of other tasks.

Mechanisms do not operate in isolation.

Their roles depend on surrounding activity, competing pathways, earlier learning, and the conditions under which they are engaged.

A feature that appears specialized may serve multiple functions. A circuit that seems stable may reorganize when the input changes. A pathway identified in one task may become irrelevant when another route can produce the same result.

The scientific problem therefore expands beyond identifying components.

It includes the arrangement connecting them.

Current interpretability methods are particularly effective at examining trained models during specific tasks. They are less complete as accounts of how the observed configuration developed and how it may change.

A trained model reflects a long sequence of optimization steps. Features emerge, interact, compete, and become integrated with previously learned patterns. Some representations stabilize early. Others appear later or are reorganized by subsequent training.

The final configuration contains the accumulated consequences of that history.

An interpretability experiment may reveal a circuit present today without revealing the sequence through which it formed.

The same limitation applies to future behavior.

A mechanism that appears reliable under current conditions may change after fine-tuning, new data, altered feedback, or continued deployment. A pathway may remain stable, become strengthened, lose influence, or be replaced by another route.

Present configuration does not automatically determine future development.

Interpretability also leaves questions of robustness unresolved.

A circuit may operate reliably for familiar inputs but fail when the context changes. Several representations may cooperate during routine tasks and interfere with one another under unusual conditions. A pathway that appears central may prove dispensable when the model finds an alternative.

Researchers can increasingly describe what occurs inside a model during selected computations.

A broader explanation must also account for:

- how internal mechanisms formed;
- how they interact across tasks;
- why some remain stable;
- why others fail;
- how training changes them;
- and what future behavior their arrangement makes possible.

Mechanistic interpretability supplies crucial evidence for answering these questions.

It does not answer them alone.

The field has begun revealing the internal structures created through learning with unprecedented precision.

The challenge that follows is not simply to discover what structures exist.

It is to understand why their arrangement produces intelligence.

Endnotes

1. Mechanistic interpretability investigates how the internal components, representations, and computational processes of trained neural networks contribute to model behavior. Rather than treating performance alone as the object of explanation, it attempts to reconstruct aspects of the computation implemented by the learned system.

2. In interpretability research, a feature generally refers to an internal direction, pattern, or representation associated with some recurring property of the information or computation being processed. Features need not correspond one-to-one with individual neurons or with concepts that have simple human-readable labels.

3. Neural representations are frequently distributed across populations of units rather than localized to a single neuron. Conversely, individual units may participate in multiple representational or computational patterns, making neuron-level interpretation alone insufficient for many forms of explanation.

4. Activation analysis examines the internal states produced while a model processes particular inputs. Comparing activation patterns across prompts, tasks, or conditions can reveal where information is represented or transformed, although observational activation evidence alone does not establish causal involvement.

5. In mechanistic interpretability, a circuit refers to a set of interacting model components that collectively implement or contribute to a recognizable computation. Research has identified relatively compact circuits for several tasks, while also showing that circuit boundaries and component roles can depend on context. See, for example, Olah et al., "Zoom In: An Introduction to Circuits" (2020).

6. Interpretability studies have reconstructed circuits for specific computations in transformer models, including induction-like pattern completion, indirect-object identification, and forms of information movement across token positions. Such results demonstrate that at least some learned computations can be decomposed into experimentally testable internal structures. See Olsson et al., "In-context Learning and Induction Heads" (2022), and Wang et al., "Interpretability in the Wild: a Circuit for Indirect Object Identification in GPT-2 small" (2023).

7. Superposition describes a representational arrangement in which more features can be encoded than can be assigned cleanly to separate neural dimensions. Multiple features may therefore share overlapping combinations of units, helping explain why individual neurons can respond to apparently unrelated properties. See Elhage et al., "Toy Models of Superposition" (2022).

8. Sparse representation methods, including sparse autoencoders, attempt to decompose dense neural activations into a larger set of latent features of which only a relatively small subset is active at a given time. These methods have become an important approach for recovering more interpretable feature representations from large language models. See Huben et al., "Sparse Autoencoders Find Highly Interpretable Features in Language Models" (2024).

9. Causal interpretability methods intervene on internal model states rather than merely observing them. Suppression, amplification, replacement, or removal of internal activity can provide stronger evidence about whether a component or representation contributes causally to an observed computation. See Geiger et al., "Causal Abstractions of Neural Networks" (2021).

10. Activation patching compares internal states across related model runs by replacing activation values in one run with corresponding values from another and measuring the resulting change in output. The method can help identify where behaviorally relevant information enters, moves through, or influences a computation. See Conmy et al., "Towards Automated Circuit Discovery for Mechanistic Interpretability" (2023).

11. Ablation tests causal dependence by disabling, removing, or suppressing a model component and observing the resulting behavioral or computational effects. An unchanged outcome does not necessarily demonstrate irrelevance, because redundancy, compensation, or alternative pathways may preserve performance.

12. Model editing refers to methods designed to alter selected knowledge, associations, representations, or behaviors within a trained model without retraining the entire system. Editing experiments can also serve as mechanistic probes because the pattern of intended and unintended changes provides evidence about how the targeted information is organized internally. See, for example, Meng et al., "Locating and Editing Factual Associations in GPT" (2022).

CHAPTER 4

Correct Answers Can Hide Wrong Mechanisms

A correct answer naturally inspires confidence.

When a student solves a difficult mathematics problem, a physician reaches the correct diagnosis, or an engineer identifies the source of a mechanical failure, success often leads us to assume that the underlying reasoning was also sound. The visible result appears to confirm the process that produced it.

Artificial intelligence encourages the same intuition.

When a language model writes a convincing explanation, produces functioning computer code, summarizes a scientific article, or answers a difficult examination question correctly, the output appears to validate the reasoning behind it.

The explanation is coherent.

The conclusion is accurate.

The result looks intelligent.

From that success, an assumption follows:

Correct behavior reflects correct internal reasoning.

A correct answer, however, identifies only the outcome of a computation. It does not reveal the computation that produced it.[1]

Imagine asking several people to estimate the height of a mountain.

One carefully applies trigonometry using measured angles and known distances. Another remembers the value from a guidebook. A third recognizes the mountain from a documentary. A fourth estimates its height by comparing it with nearby peaks.

Each person may provide exactly the same number.

The agreement tells us nothing about how the answer was obtained.

One answer emerged from calculation.

Another came from memory.

Another from recognition.

Another from approximation.

The visible result is identical, but the processes producing it are not.[2]

Artificial intelligence presents the same problem.

A model may generate an accurate legal summary because it identified the relevant principles, distinguished the competing claims, and reconstructed the structure of the argument. Another may produce the same summary by matching the document to recurring patterns in similar legal texts. A third may combine fragments of retrieved language that happen to converge on a correct conclusion.

From the outside, all three outputs may appear equally successful.

The response does not identify the mechanism responsible for the success.

A system may solve a problem through a durable reasoning strategy. It may also succeed through an incomplete strategy that happens to produce the same answer.

The outcome alone cannot distinguish between them.

Human evaluation frequently encounters the same limitation.

A multiple-choice response reveals which option was selected. It does not reveal whether the person derived the answer, remembered it, eliminated the alternatives, misunderstood the question but guessed correctly, or copied the result from another source.

The score records success.

It does not explain it.

A correct answer is therefore not the end of an investigation.

For increasingly capable artificial intelligence systems, it is often the beginning.

4.1 One Behavior, Many Causes

The ambiguity runs in both directions.

The same correct answer can arise from different mechanisms.

The same incorrect answer can arise from different failures.

Suppose two language models answer the same scientific question incorrectly.

One model may never have encoded the relevant information.

Another may contain the correct information but fail to retrieve it.

A third may retrieve the necessary facts but combine them incorrectly.

A fourth may activate several competing representations and allow an irrelevant association to dominate the final response.

The recorded failure is the same.

The underlying causes are not.[3]

This difference matters because interventions must address causes rather than appearances.

A model that lacks information may require new training data.

A model that contains the information but cannot retrieve it may require a different form of access or prompting.

A model disrupted by competing representations may require changes to the computation that selects among them.

A model that applies the wrong relationship may require correction of the internal representation itself.

The same outward failure can therefore require entirely different solutions.

Consider two systems asked to predict the result of a scientific experiment.

One identifies the causal relationship among the variables and uses that relationship to derive the answer.

The other recognizes that the arrangement resembles examples encountered during training and reproduces the result usually associated with that pattern.

For the original experiment, both systems may be correct.

Now rearrange the variables while preserving the underlying causal principle.

The first system can reconstruct the answer.

The second may continue following the old surface pattern.

From the outside, the original responses appeared identical.

Internally, the models were solving different problems.

Observable behavior is therefore **mechanistically underdetermined**.[4]

A single output is compatible with multiple internal explanations.

Neither correctness nor failure uniquely identifies its cause.

Evaluation must therefore treat an output as evidence compatible with several possible internal explanations.

The task is not simply to determine whether the model succeeded.

It is to determine which internal process best explains the success or failure.

Figure 2 illustrates this central ambiguity: the same observable result can arise from fundamentally different internal routes.

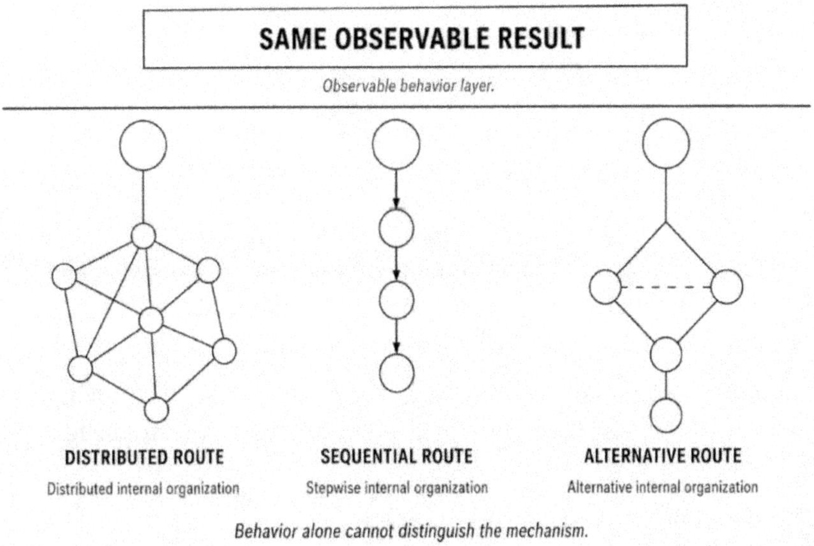

Figure 2. Different Mechanisms Can Produce the Same Observable Result.

From the outside, systems may appear almost identical.

Internally, they may be solving different problems.

4.2 What Benchmarks Measure

Standardized benchmarks made modern artificial intelligence measurable.

They provided common tasks through which researchers could compare systems objectively. Models could be evaluated on the same images, questions, programming problems, scientific examinations, and reasoning tasks.

Performance became quantifiable.

Improvements became easier to detect.

Comparisons became more reliable.

Without benchmarks, progress across rapidly evolving systems would be difficult to assess consistently.

Yet every benchmark answers a bounded question:

Did the model succeed under these conditions?[5]

It does not answer:

Why did the model succeed?

A benchmark evaluates observable performance.

It cannot directly identify the internal process responsible for that performance.

Every benchmark defines an environment.

It specifies the task, the input format, the information available, and the criteria used to determine success. Within those boundaries, performance can be measured with great precision.

But the score does not reveal whether the model relied on a principle that extends beyond the test or on a strategy closely fitted to the test itself.

This does not mean benchmarks are flawed.

It means they measure exactly what they were designed to measure.

A blood-pressure reading measures blood pressure.

It does not diagnose the disease producing it.

Likewise, a benchmark measures performance.

It does not identify the computational process responsible for that performance.

Two models may receive the same score while relying on very different internal strategies.

One may represent the underlying relationships required by the task.

Another may depend on regularities specific to the benchmark's format or examples.

As long as those regularities remain available, both systems appear equally capable.

A change in the evaluation conditions can expose the difference.[6]

As **Figure 3** shows, equivalent benchmark performance can conceal very different internal organizations whose differences become visible only when the conditions change.

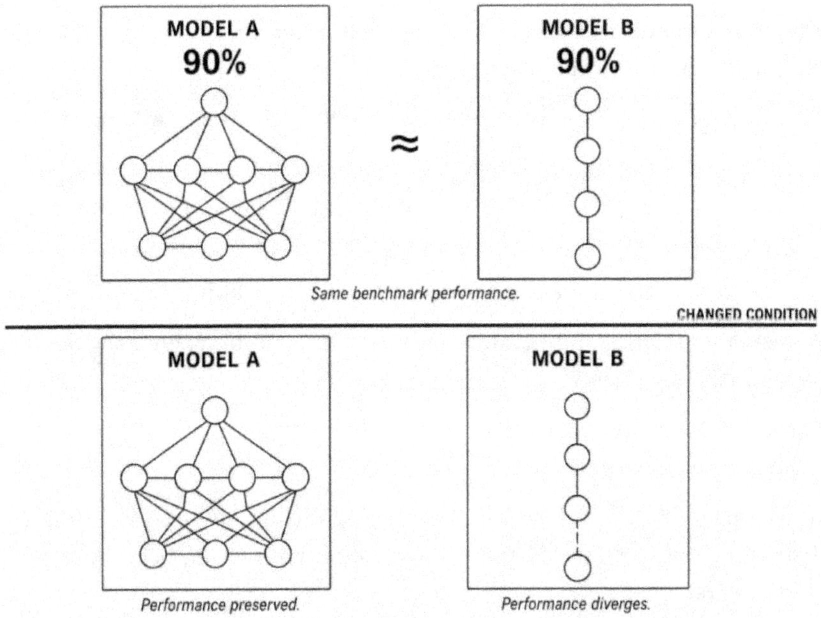

Figure 3. Same Performance, Different Internal Organization.

Researchers may reformulate a question, introduce irrelevant information, alter the order of the evidence, require several steps instead of one, combine previously separate concepts, or present a familiar principle in an unfamiliar context.

These tests do not merely ask the model for more answers.

They test whether the process producing the answers remains stable.

A model may solve a mathematical problem when it appears in familiar symbolic notation, then fail when the same relationship is presented geometrically or described in ordinary language.

A programming model may generate correct code for a familiar library but struggle when the same algorithm must be implemented in an unfamiliar environment.

A legal system may identify the correct rule in a standard case but fail when several precedents interact in a new configuration.

The original benchmark result was genuine.

It simply did not determine whether the strategy supporting that result would remain dependable beyond the tested conditions.

Scientific evaluation must therefore test the stability of the process, not only the accuracy of the result.

This requires more than increasing the number of benchmark questions.

A larger test may still reproduce the same assumptions, formats, and statistical regularities. If the environment remains unchanged, the evaluation may continue rewarding the same narrow strategy.

More examples do not necessarily create a different kind of evidence.

A deeper evaluation deliberately changes the conditions under which the capability must operate.[7]

It asks whether the model can preserve the relevant relationship while surface details change.

It examines whether a result survives paraphrasing, missing information, distracting cues, altered formats, novel combinations, and competing alternatives.

Such tests do not reveal the complete internal mechanism.

They do, however, constrain the possible explanations.

A strategy that survives meaningful variation is less likely to depend on a narrow cue.

A strategy that collapses after a superficial change reveals something about the process that produced the earlier success.

Benchmarks remain essential.

But a score should be treated as evidence of performance within a defined environment, not as proof of the mechanism underlying that performance.

4.3 Reliability Requires Mechanistic Evidence

Reliability depends on more than repeated success.

It depends on whether the process producing that success remains stable when the demands placed upon it change.

A bridge is not considered safe merely because it remained standing yesterday. Engineers examine the forces acting through its structure, the materials carrying those forces, and the conditions under which failure could occur.

Previous success matters.

The mechanism supporting that success matters more when future conditions cannot be controlled.

Artificial intelligence increasingly requires the same standard.

A model may perform accurately across thousands of cases while depending on a process that is vulnerable to one untested change. The weakness may remain invisible until the system is placed in a situation where the original regularity no longer holds.

Repeated success provides evidence.

Mechanistic explanation provides confidence.

This difference becomes critical when systems operate in medicine, science, engineering, finance, law, education, or public decision-making. In such settings, reliability cannot mean that the model was usually correct under previous conditions.

It must also address why the model was correct, what computational pathway supported the result, and how that pathway responds when the situation changes.

A wrong answer may reflect missing knowledge, failed retrieval, interference, incorrect transformation, or unstable selection.

A correct answer may reflect causal understanding, remembered association, pattern recognition, elimination, or coincidence.

AI evaluation must therefore connect capability with the mechanisms that sustain it. Reliability depends not only on past accuracy, but on whether the supporting process remains stable when conditions change. That requires evidence about the organization beneath the score and the circumstances under which its dependability ends.

ENDNOTES

1. Observable performance and internal mechanism are distinct forms of evidence. A model's output establishes what occurred under a particular set of conditions, but the same observable result can be compatible with different representations, computational pathways, or strategies. Determining which process produced the result requires additional evidence about the model's internal organization.

2. Machine-learning systems can arrive at similar outputs through substantially different internal strategies. One system may rely on a representation that captures the underlying structure of a task, while another may exploit a statistical regularity, memorized association, or context-specific shortcut. Behavioral agreement therefore does not imply mechanistic equivalence.

3. Similar failures can arise at different stages of computation. Relevant information may be absent, represented but not retrieved, retrieved but transformed incorrectly, disrupted by competing representations, or available to the system but not selected for the final response. Distinguishing among these possibilities requires evidence beyond the outward error itself.

4. Mechanistic underdetermination refers here to the fact that an observed behavior does not uniquely specify the internal process that generated it. Multiple candidate mechanisms may remain compatible with the same behavioral evidence. The use of this principle as the basis for a structured diagnostic framework is a central conceptual development of this book.

5. Benchmarks evaluate performance on defined tasks, datasets, prompts, scoring procedures, and conditions. They are indispensable for comparing capabilities, but a benchmark score does not by itself determine which internal strategy produced the performance or whether that strategy will remain reliable outside the tested distribution.

6. Research on robustness, distribution shift, shortcut learning, and out-of-distribution generalization has shown that strong performance under one set of conditions may deteriorate when superficial correlations, input formats, contextual cues, or environmental regularities change. Such changes can reveal dependencies that were not apparent in the original evaluation.

7. Robustness testing commonly varies prompts, contexts, distributions, perturbations, or task conditions to determine whether a capability persists beyond the circumstances in which it was originally measured. The broader interpretation developed in this book is that such evidence should also be used to constrain hypotheses about the internal mechanism supporting the capability, rather than being treated only as another performance score.

PART II

From Engineering to Scientific Investigation

Modern artificial intelligence presents a new kind of scientific problem.

Learning creates forms of internal organization that cannot be understood completely from architecture, training procedures, or external performance alone. As trained systems became increasingly accessible to internal investigation, the task expanded beyond building capable models toward explaining the organization that learning had produced.

That transition raises a new question.

How should a science of learned intelligence be conducted?

Scientific progress requires more than increasingly detailed observations of internal structures. It requires methods for distinguishing mechanisms from correlations, connecting observations into explanations, and identifying organizational principles that generalize across different learned systems.

The deeper shift is therefore not simply from engineering to science, but from observation to explanation.

A science of learned intelligence will ultimately be judged not by how much it can see inside a model, but by how well it can explain why organized computation emerges, remains stable, changes, and sometimes fails.

CHAPTER 5

When Intelligence Becomes a Scientific Object

5.1 When Building Comes Before Science

For much of history, engineering and science did not advance in the order we often imagine.

Today it is easy to assume that scientific understanding comes first, followed by technological application. Scientists discover fundamental principles, engineers apply those principles, and new technologies emerge from that knowledge.

History has often unfolded differently.

People frequently learned how to build useful systems before they fully understood the principles governing their behavior.

The early steam engine is one of the clearest examples.

Long before thermodynamics existed as a mature science, engineers had already developed machines capable of pumping water from mines, powering factories, and transforming industry.[1] These engines became increasingly reliable through practical experience, experimentation, and incremental improvement.

Yet an important question remained unanswered.

Why did they work as they did?

Engineers could modify designs, improve efficiency, and solve practical problems, but they lacked a general account of the relationships among heat, energy, work, and efficiency. Those broader principles emerged only later through the development of thermodynamics.

The arrival of a mature science did not replace engineering.

It explained what engineering had already made possible.

The scientific questions were different from the engineering ones.

An engineer might ask how to produce a more efficient engine.

A scientist might ask why certain designs consistently performed better, what general principles governed energy transfer, which observations reflected universal laws rather than individual machines, and how those laws could explain systems that had not yet been built.

Engineering created the object.

Science sought to explain it.

Artificial intelligence may now be approaching a similar transition.

For decades, progress in AI has been driven primarily by engineering. Researchers have developed increasingly powerful architectures, assembled larger datasets, designed more effective optimization procedures, and expanded the computational resources available for training. These advances have produced systems capable of remarkable performance across language, vision, reasoning, programming, and scientific discovery.

Their success has created a new situation.

Modern AI systems are no longer interesting only because they perform useful tasks. Learning has produced internal organizations whose properties cannot be completely inferred from the design process alone.[2]

At the beginning of development, a model is an engineering project. Researchers choose an architecture, define an objective, prepare training data, and establish the procedures through which learning will occur.

After training, the resulting system can be observed, compared, manipulated, and explained.

This is what distinguishes a scientific object.[3]

A scientific object is not simply something that attracts scientific interest. It is a system whose properties raise questions that cannot be answered completely from knowledge of its construction alone. Its behavior must be observed. Its mechanisms must be inferred from evidence. Its responses must be tested under changing conditions. Its recurring patterns must be compared across many instances before broader principles can emerge.

The trained AI model now possesses these characteristics.

The model remains an engineered mathematical system produced through intentionally designed training procedures. Yet the organization created through learning has become an empirical phenomenon in its own right.

Its learned representations can be investigated.

Its unexpected capabilities can become scientific observations.

Its failures can provide evidence about the organization that produced them.

Its responses to new conditions can reveal recurring properties of learned intelligence.

The model is no longer only the result of engineering.

It has become something science must explain.

5.2 Engineering Questions and Scientific Questions

Once a technology becomes a scientific object, the questions surrounding it begin to change.

Engineering is primarily concerned with creating systems that achieve desired goals. It asks how a system can be designed, improved, optimized, and deployed more effectively. Success may be measured through greater capability, higher efficiency, lower cost, faster training, or broader applicability.

Scientific investigation pursues a different objective.

Its purpose is not simply to improve a system but to explain it.[4] Scientific questions seek mechanisms, principles, and regularities that extend beyond any individual example. They ask not only whether something works, but why it works, how it works, under what conditions it changes, and which observations reflect broader principles rather than isolated events.

These are complementary forms of knowledge.

An engineer developing a language model may ask which architecture produces stronger reasoning, which optimization strategy accelerates learning, or which training procedure improves mathematical performance.

A scientist may ask different questions.

What internal representations supported that improvement?

Which mechanisms changed during learning?

Would the same mechanisms emerge if the model were trained again?

Do similar capabilities consistently rely on similar forms of organization, or can they arise through fundamentally different internal solutions?

These questions do not compete with engineering.

They begin where engineering succeeds.

During development, researchers choose the architecture, prepare the data, define the objective, and establish how learning will occur. Each of these decisions belongs to engineering design.

Once training is complete, however, the resulting model contains properties that cannot be fully described by those decisions alone.

Learning has created an internal organization that must be examined on its own terms.

5.3 The Trained Model as Evidence

The trained model occupies an unusual position.

It is simultaneously the **product of engineering** and the **source of scientific evidence**.

Every learned representation provides evidence about how information became organized.

Every unexpected capability provides evidence about what learning can produce under particular conditions.

Every failure provides evidence about the limits of the mechanisms supporting successful behavior.

Every difference between trained models provides evidence about the range of organizations capable of producing similar capabilities.

This changes the meaning of observation.

When an engineer observes that a model has become better at solving mathematical problems, the result naturally raises questions about improving future systems.

A scientist can begin with the same observation and ask:

What changed inside the model?

Which internal representations became more effective?

Did existing mechanisms become more efficient, or did new ones emerge?

Can those changes be reproduced across other architectures?

Do they reflect a general property of learning or a distinctive consequence of one training history?

The observation is identical.

The questions are different.

Unexpected behavior also acquires a different scientific meaning.

A surprising capability is not merely a feature to celebrate. It raises questions about which conditions allowed that capability to emerge, whether it depends on mechanisms shared with other tasks, and whether similar capabilities appear in independently trained systems.

A failure is not merely a defect to eliminate. It can reveal the boundaries of a learned strategy, expose competition among internal processes, or identify conditions under which an apparently stable capability breaks down.[5]

Variation among models is not merely inconsistency. It can show how many different internal arrangements are capable of supporting similar behavior.

The trained system therefore provides more than performance.

It provides evidence about the processes through which learned intelligence becomes organized.

5.4 From Individual Findings to General Principles

Observation is the beginning of science.

It is not its destination.

Recent advances in mechanistic interpretability have begun to reveal individual features, computational circuits, activation patterns, and learned representations within trained models.[6] These discoveries provide direct observations of internal organization that previously remained inaccessible.

Each discovery expands knowledge of a particular system.

A mature science must determine which findings extend beyond the model in which they were discovered.

Does the same mechanism emerge repeatedly across independently trained models?

Do certain capabilities consistently depend on similar forms of internal organization?

Are some representations common across architectures, while others reflect particular datasets or training procedures?

Do recurring developmental patterns appear as models acquire increasingly complex abilities?

Which mechanisms are specific to one model, and which reflect more general properties of learned intelligence?

These questions move beyond describing a single system.

An observation tells us something about a particular model.

A scientific principle explains why comparable observations appear across many models.

Suppose researchers identify a computational circuit that contributes to mathematical reasoning in one language model.

That finding immediately generates further questions.

Does a comparable circuit emerge in other models?

Does it appear in different architectures?

Does it develop gradually during training or emerge abruptly?

Does it remain stable after additional learning?

Can similar organizational patterns support different capabilities?

Each answer extends knowledge beyond the original observation.

Gradually, isolated discoveries connect into a broader picture.

Relationships emerge between mechanisms.

Patterns become reproducible.

Hypotheses become testable.

General principles begin replacing isolated descriptions.

Interpretability research is producing an expanding collection of observations about learned systems. The larger scientific challenge is to determine which observations reflect general characteristics of learned intelligence and which remain specific to individual architectures, datasets, or training histories.

This requires comparison across models rather than explanation of one model alone.

It requires experiments designed not merely to identify a mechanism, but to determine whether that mechanism recurs, how it develops, when it changes, and what range of behavior it can support.

It requires theories capable of connecting internal organization with learning history, computation, stability, and variation.

Progress can no longer be measured only by increasingly capable systems.

It must also be measured by increasingly powerful explanations.

A broader scientific enterprise is therefore beginning to take shape—one devoted to explaining the organization, development, and governing principles of learned intelligence.

If artificial intelligence has become a scientific object, what kind of science is best prepared to study it?

ENDNOTES

1. The development of the steam engine preceded the mature formulation of thermodynamics. Early engines were developed and improved through engineering practice before nineteenth-century work on heat, work, energy, and efficiency produced the theoretical framework that became classical thermodynamics. The example illustrates a broader historical pattern in which practical construction can precede comprehensive scientific explanation.

2. Modern machine-learning systems are intentionally designed at the level of architecture, objectives, optimization procedures, data, and training conditions, but many of the representations and computational strategies present in the trained system emerge through learning rather than being specified individually in advance. Investigating the trained organization therefore requires empirical methods in addition to knowledge of how the system was constructed.

3. The term *scientific object* is used in this book operationally to describe a learned system whose properties must be investigated empirically rather than inferred completely from its construction. In this sense, the trained model becomes an object of observation, comparison, causal intervention, explanation, and generalization. This usage forms part of the conceptual framework developed in the book rather than a formal classification universally adopted in artificial-intelligence research.

4. Engineering and scientific explanation often address different but complementary questions. Engineering primarily seeks reliable construction, optimization, control, and performance, whereas scientific explanation seeks mechanisms, causal relationships, regularities, and principles that account for why systems behave as they do and under what conditions those explanations remain valid.

5. Errors, unexpected behaviors, and differences among trained models can provide scientifically useful evidence about learned organization. Changes in performance across contexts or perturbations can reveal the limits of a strategy, identify dependencies among internal processes, and constrain hypotheses about which mechanisms support a capability.

6. Mechanistic interpretability research has increasingly identified internal features, activation patterns, computational circuits, and causally relevant components in trained neural networks. Most such findings initially concern particular models, tasks, or experimental settings. The broader program proposed in this book asks which findings reproduce across independently trained systems, how they arise through development, and when they support more general principles of learned intelligence.

CHAPTER 6

What Neuroscience Brings

6.1 Why Neuroscience Became Necessary

For centuries, the brain was studied without the existence of neuroscience.

Anatomists described its visible structures. Physiologists investigated electrical activity, sensory pathways, reflexes, and motor control. Physicians documented the symptoms produced by injury and disease. Each field revealed important aspects of the nervous system, yet none could fully explain how perception, memory, language, reasoning, or conscious experience emerged from its coordinated activity.

The difficulty was not a lack of observations.

It was a mismatch between the questions being asked and the complexity of the system being studied.

Anatomy could identify structures without explaining the cognitive processes they supported. Physiology could measure electrical responses without showing how those responses became perception or thought. Clinical observation could associate damage with impairment without revealing the complete network of processes that had been disrupted.

Understanding cognition required a science capable of connecting these levels.

Researchers needed to study not only what structures existed or where activity occurred, but how information moved, how interactions changed over time, how prior experience altered future processing, and how coherent behavior emerged from many processes operating together.

Neuroscience developed around this explanatory challenge.[1]

Its importance did not come from replacing anatomy, physiology, psychology, or medicine. It came from bringing their observations into a common investigation of organized cognition.

Artificial intelligence now presents a related problem. Architecture, optimization, data, and computation explain how models are built and trained, but not fully how learned organization supports complex behavior.

The relevance of neuroscience is methodological rather than biological. Artificial intelligence is not a brain, but both fields confront the problem of explaining cognition produced through interactions among many components.

Neuroscience therefore contributes more than biological facts. It provides principles for investigating systems in which function depends on causal interaction, changing internal states, developmental history, and multiple possible forms of organization.

6.2 Activity Is Not Function

One of the most important lessons in neuroscience is that activity alone does not identify function.[2]

A neuron or brain region may become active during a task without producing the process being studied. Its activity may reflect information arriving from elsewhere, preparation for a later response, feedback from another system, or a consequence of a computation that has already occurred.

Correlation can identify where investigation should begin.

It cannot establish what role a component played.

This limitation became increasingly important as methods for recording neural activity improved. Researchers could observe neurons responding to particular stimuli, actions, faces, locations, sounds, or decisions. Some responses appeared remarkably selective, encouraging the idea that the active cell or region might contain the function itself.

But selectivity is not explanation.

A neuron that responds when a person recognizes a face may contribute to recognition, receive the outcome of recognition, signal its relevance to another process, or participate only under a narrow set of conditions. The same recorded activity can be consistent with several causal roles.

Neuroscience addresses this ambiguity through intervention.

Lesion studies provided one of the earliest forms of causal evidence. When injury to a particular structure was followed by a specific impairment, researchers could infer that the damaged tissue had contributed to the lost function.

A lesion may damage several neighboring structures, interrupt pathways connecting distant regions, alter the balance of the remaining network, or trigger compensatory changes over time. The observed impairment therefore reflects not only what was removed but how the rest of the system responded to its absence.

A damaged component may have been necessary for the task under ordinary conditions. That does not mean it performed the entire function by itself.

Electrical and magnetic stimulation offered a different kind of evidence.[3] By increasing or disrupting activity in a selected region, researchers could observe whether perception, movement, memory, or decision-making changed.

Stimulation can show that altering a component influences a process.

It does not automatically reveal the natural computation that the component normally performs. Artificially activating a region may recruit pathways differently from ordinary cognition, and the resulting effect may depend on timing, intensity, and the state of the surrounding network.

Necessity and sufficiency must therefore be distinguished.[4]

If disrupting a component prevents a function, it may be necessary in that context. If activating it produces or biases the function, it may be sufficient to influence the process.

Neither result alone provides a complete mechanism.

A component may be necessary but not sufficient because it performs only one step within a larger process. It may appear sufficient under artificial stimulation even though ordinary cognition usually reaches the same result through a broader pathway. It may be necessary in one context but replaceable in another.

Causal explanation requires convergence.

Recording shows when activity appears.

Lesions reveal what is lost when part of the system is damaged.

Stimulation reveals what changes when activity is altered.

Behavioral testing identifies the conditions under which the effect occurs.

Network analysis examines how the intervention changes communication elsewhere.

Together, these methods narrow the range of possible mechanisms.

The same causal discipline applies to artificial intelligence.

Discovering that a feature or circuit becomes active during a task does not establish that it performs the task. Disrupting it may reveal causal dependence, but the effect must still be interpreted within the larger computation. Another pathway may compensate. The intervention may alter several functions at once. A mechanism that appears essential for one prompt may be unnecessary when the same problem is presented differently.

The central question is:

What causal role did that activity play within the organized computation?

Neuroscience brings a disciplined way of separating observation from participation, participation from necessity, and necessity from complete explanation.

6.3 Cognition Depends on System State

The same neural component does not always perform the same function in the same way.

Its contribution depends partly on the state of the larger system.

Attention can strengthen the response to one stimulus while suppressing another. Expectation can alter how ambiguous information is interpreted. Prior learning can change which features become salient. Current goals can recruit one pathway while leaving another relatively inactive. Fatigue, arousal, uncertainty, and competing demands can reshape processing without changing the underlying anatomy.

The stimulus may remain the same.

The system receiving it does not.

Neuroscience therefore studies cognition as a dynamic process rather than a fixed map of functions.[5]

Imagine presenting the same faint visual signal under two conditions. In one, the observer has been told where the signal is likely to appear. In the other, attention is directed elsewhere.

The sensory input may be nearly identical, yet neural processing and conscious detection can differ. The difference cannot be explained by the stimulus alone. It depends on the state of the system before and during the event.

Expectation produces a related effect.

When the brain receives incomplete information, prior beliefs and recent context influence how that information is interpreted. A sound embedded in one sequence may be heard differently when placed in another. An ambiguous image may take on a different meaning after a relevant cue. The internal state establishes which interpretation receives support.

This makes context part of the mechanism rather than background noise.

An activity pattern observed under one condition cannot automatically be assigned a permanent, context-free function. Researchers must ask whether the same pattern appears across tasks, goals, environments, levels of attention, and stages of learning.

Variation becomes evidence.

If a component contributes only when attention is directed toward a stimulus, its function cannot be described independently of attention. If a pathway becomes important only under uncertainty, uncertainty is part of the explanation. If a region changes its role after practice, the function belongs not only to the region but to the state and history of the wider network.

The same principle applies to learned artificial systems.

An internal feature may strongly influence an answer under one prompt and contribute little under another. A pathway may support factual retrieval when the context is clear but compete with other associations when the prompt is ambiguous. A mechanism may appear reliable during routine processing yet become unstable when irrelevant information, conflicting cues, or unfamiliar combinations alter the system's internal state.

The relevant questions therefore include:

Under what conditions does this mechanism operate?

Which surrounding activity gives it its current role?

What changes when the system enters a different state?

Does the mechanism remain stable when attention, context, uncertainty, or task demands change?

A component cannot be understood entirely in isolation from the state that makes its activity meaningful.

6.4 Development Must Be Studied in Time

A mature nervous system reveals what organization exists now.

It does not reveal how that organization formed.

Neuroscience therefore investigates development as a process unfolding over time. Researchers do not rely only on comparisons between fully developed systems. They follow changes across stages, examine when particular capacities emerge, identify periods of heightened plasticity, and study how early experience alters later organization.

Longitudinal research is especially valuable because it tracks the same system across time.[6]

A cross-sectional comparison may show that younger and older individuals differ. A longitudinal study can reveal how the difference developed: which changes appeared first, which remained stable, which accelerated, and which depended on earlier events.

Sequence becomes evidence.

Suppose a neural representation is present in a mature system. Examining only the final state cannot determine whether it appeared early and remained stable, emerged gradually through repeated experience, or replaced an earlier organization.

Those histories may produce similar present behavior while implying different mechanisms of learning.

Critical periods provide another example.

During some developmental windows, experience can produce effects that become harder to reproduce later. The system is not equally plastic at every moment.[7] Its ability to reorganize depends on its current stage, existing connections, and prior exposure.

Development therefore cannot always be treated as the accumulation of interchangeable updates. Timing matters.

The same experience may produce different consequences depending on when it occurs.

Plasticity research extends this principle beyond early development. Learning, injury, practice, and environmental change can reorganize neural responses throughout life, but the form and extent of that reorganization depend on the system's existing structure.

New learning acts upon a system that has already been shaped.

The methodological lesson extends beyond the fact that training history matters: history itself can be investigated experimentally.

Researchers can examine models at multiple stages of training rather than only after completion. They can identify when a representation first becomes detectable, when separate features begin to interact, when one pathway becomes dominant, or when a fragile shortcut gives way to a more general strategy.

They can compare learning trajectories rather than only final performance.

Two models that end with similar capabilities may have reached them through different developmental paths. One mechanism may emerge early and organize later learning around itself. Another may appear only after competing strategies have weakened. A later intervention may have different effects depending on which trajectory produced the current organization.

The present system is therefore not only a configuration.

It is a temporary state within an unfolding developmental trajectory.

Studying that trajectory can reveal mechanisms that the final state conceals.

6.5 Degeneracy: Similar Function, Different Organization

Chapter 4 established that similar behavior can conceal different mechanisms. Neuroscience studies one important form of that problem through the concept of **degeneracy**.

Degeneracy occurs when structurally different components or pathways can support similar functions.[8] It is not simply duplication. Two mechanisms need not be identical copies of one another. They may use different structures, signals, or routes while producing comparable outcomes.

This property is common in complex biological systems.

Two individuals may perform the same cognitive task successfully while relying on somewhat different patterns of neural recruitment. The differences may reflect development, practice, strategy, anatomy, or previous experience.

Degeneracy becomes especially visible after disruption.

When one pathway is damaged, another may partially assume its role. Recovery may occur because the original mechanism was restored, because a neighboring process expanded, because a previously secondary route became dominant, or because the individual adopted a new strategy that reached a similar behavioral result.

The recovered function may look familiar from the outside.

Internally, it may now depend on a different organization.

This is not the same as simple redundancy.

Redundant systems contain duplicate components capable of performing essentially the same operation. Degenerate systems can produce the same functional outcome through components that are structurally or computationally different.

The distinction matters because compensation may preserve behavior while changing the mechanism beneath it.

Neuroscience investigates degeneracy by comparing individuals, measuring changes before and after injury or learning, disrupting candidate pathways, and examining whether alternative routes become active. Researchers ask not only whether the function survives, but how it survives.

For AI science, degeneracy raises several questions.

Do independently trained models develop the same solution to a task, or merely solutions that behave similarly?

If one pathway is disrupted, does another reproduce the same computation or compensate through a different one?

Does fine-tuning restore the original mechanism, reorganize the task around an alternative route, or create a new strategy that passes the same evaluation?

Can two models with similar capabilities differ in their vulnerability to future changes because their internal organizations are not the same?

Degeneracy therefore changes what counts as an explanation.

Identifying one mechanism that supports a capability does not prove that the mechanism is universal or uniquely required. The same function may be realizable through several organizations, each with different strengths, limitations, and possible futures.

6.6 What Neuroscience Changes About AI Science

Neuroscience directs attention toward four connected questions.

First, what causal role does an observed component play?

Does it participate in producing the capability, or does its activity merely accompany a process occurring elsewhere?

Second, under what state does that role appear?

How does the component's contribution change when context, uncertainty, competing information, or task demands alter the wider system?

Third, how did the mechanism develop?

Through what sequence of learning did it emerge, and could a different developmental path have produced another organization?

Finally, is the mechanism uniquely required?

Is it the only route capable of supporting the function, or one of several possible internal solutions?

These questions require a different level of explanation from a static inventory of features and circuits.

A feature may be causally important only within a particular state.

A mechanism observed after training may conceal several earlier stages through which it developed.

A successful intervention may preserve behavior by recruiting a different organization rather than restoring the original process.

The object of investigation is therefore not an isolated component.

It is the component's role within an organized system operating under particular conditions and carrying a particular history.

Time is also central to explanation.

Cognition unfolds through sequences of activity. Information is selected, transformed, compared, and redirected. The role of one process depends on what occurred before it and what follows afterward.

A static observation may identify the components present during a computation.

Understanding requires reconstructing how their interactions produce the result.

Neuroscience has spent decades confronting this difficulty. It has learned that cognition cannot be fully explained by anatomy alone, activity alone, a single causal intervention, or a catalog of specialized parts.

Explanations must connect structure, activity, state, history, causality, and variation.

Artificial intelligence now requires the same depth of questioning.[9]

The challenge is no longer merely to see inside a model. Internal visibility has already begun.

The harder task is to determine how visible components become an organized computation—how their roles depend on one another, how those roles change over time, and why their interaction produces one form of behavior rather than another.

What kinds of scientific methods, conceptual tools, and explanatory strategies are required to move from seeing the parts of intelligence to understanding how they work together?

ENDNOTES

1. Modern neuroscience developed by integrating evidence across anatomy, physiology, psychology, development, clinical observation, and experimental intervention. Understanding cognition generally requires relating activity at multiple levels rather than assigning complex functions to isolated structures or measurements.

2. Neural activity observed during a task does not by itself establish the causal function of the active neuron, population, or brain region. Recorded activity may contribute directly to a computation, reflect information received from elsewhere, signal the consequence of another process, or participate only under particular conditions. Establishing function therefore requires evidence beyond correlation or selectivity.

3. Lesion, electrical-stimulation, and noninvasive brain-stimulation studies provide forms of causal evidence by altering neural systems and observing the resulting changes in behavior or processing. Their interpretation nevertheless requires caution because interventions can affect neighboring structures, connected pathways, network state, and compensatory processes in addition to the component directly targeted. For representative causal-intervention evidence, see Silvanto et al., "Baseline Cortical Excitability Determines Whether TMS Disrupts or Facilitates Behavior" (2008).

4. Necessity and sufficiency represent distinct forms of causal evidence. Disrupting a component and impairing a function can support the conclusion that the component is necessary under the tested conditions, whereas activating a component and producing or biasing an outcome can support claims about sufficiency or causal influence. Neither result alone establishes the complete mechanism through which the function is ordinarily produced.

5. Neural processing depends strongly on the state of the wider system. Attention, expectation, arousal, goals, prior learning, context, uncertainty, and competing demands can alter the contribution of the same sensory input or neural component. Functional interpretation therefore often requires specifying the conditions under which an observed activity pattern occurs. See Silvanto et al., "Baseline Cortical Excitability Determines Whether TMS Disrupts or Facilitates Behavior" (2008).

6. Longitudinal approaches follow change within the same system over time and can therefore reveal developmental sequence in ways that cross-sectional comparisons cannot. They can distinguish mechanisms that appeared early and remained stable from those that emerged gradually, reorganized, or replaced earlier forms of organization.

7. Neural plasticity varies across developmental stages and prior experience. Critical or sensitive periods demonstrate that similar experiences can have different consequences depending on when they occur, while research on lifelong plasticity shows that learning, practice, injury, and environmental change can continue reorganizing neural systems after early development. New experience therefore acts upon an organization already shaped by its history. See Draganski et al., "Changes in Grey Matter Induced by Training" (2004), and Nudo et al., "Neural Substrates for the Effects of Rehabilitative Training on Motor Recovery after Ischemic Infarct" (1996).

8. Degeneracy refers to the capacity of structurally or functionally different components or mechanisms to produce similar outcomes. It differs from simple redundancy, in which duplicate or closely equivalent components perform essentially the same operation. Degeneracy is widespread in biological systems and helps explain how similar behavior can arise from different organizations or be preserved through alternative mechanisms after disruption. See Edelman and Gally, "Degeneracy and Complexity in Biological Systems" (2001).

9. The extension of these neuroscience principles to artificial intelligence is a methodological synthesis developed in this book. It does not imply biological equivalence between brains and artificial neural networks. The proposed transfer concerns scientific reasoning: separating activity from causal function, interpreting mechanisms in relation to system state, reconstructing developmental history, testing alternative organizations, and following change through intervention and time.

CHAPTER 7

Beyond Seeing: Understanding

Interpretability has made portions of learned systems increasingly visible. Researchers can identify representations, trace limited pathways, and observe internal activity that once remained inaccessible.

Yet visibility does not by itself produce understanding.[1]

Finding an internal feature does not explain the computation in which it participates. Identifying a pathway does not reveal why information followed that route rather than another. Observing a representation does not show how it contributes to the larger process responsible for a capability.

A model containing one thousand identified features is not necessarily better understood than a model containing one hundred. A more detailed inventory may increase what researchers can observe without explaining how the observed elements work together.

Instead of asking only:

Which components are present?

Researchers must also ask:

How do those components work together to produce a computation?

Understanding begins when internal observations can be connected to the processes they collectively create.

7.1 Function Emerges Through Interaction

The functional meaning of a learned representation cannot be established in complete isolation.

Its contribution depends on what information it receives, how it interacts with other representations, how those interactions modify it, and what influence it has on later processing. The role of an individual component is therefore defined partly by its relationships within the larger organization.[2]

Consider written language.

Individual letters possess recognizable forms, yet a single letter rarely conveys a complete idea. Meaning begins to emerge as letters combine into words, words into sentences, and sentences into larger arguments. Rearranging the same letters produces different words. Rearranging the same words produces different meanings.

The important property is not the existence of the individual symbols.

It is the organization of their interactions.

An isolated feature within an artificial intelligence system may encode information about syntax, factual knowledge, visual structure, or numerical relationships. Yet that representation acquires computational significance only through its participation in a larger process.

Information is combined, transformed, strengthened, suppressed, redirected, and integrated as computation progresses through the network.

A scientific account cannot stop after identifying which representations become active. It must explain how those representations cooperate, compete, modify one another, and collectively transform information into a coherent result.

Some interactions reinforce one possibility.

Others suppress alternatives.

Some preserve information across many stages of processing.

Others temporarily reshape it into a form that allows later operations to proceed.

Removing one interaction may have little effect when another pathway can perform a similar role. Strengthening one representation may alter many later computations by changing the information available to them. A component's influence therefore cannot always be inferred from its individual properties.

Interaction itself becomes part of the explanation.[3]

7.2 Computation Unfolds Through Sequence

The interactions that produce intelligence do not occur simultaneously.

They unfold through an organized sequence.[4]

This sequence is different from the developmental process through which training created the model. The concern here is how an already trained system produces a single computation.

Every response develops through successive transformations.

Information is received, interpreted, compared, reorganized, integrated with other signals, and progressively refined. Each stage depends on what has already occurred while shaping the stages that follow.

Reasoning therefore cannot be understood as a static property stored somewhere inside the model.

It is an organized process.

Imagine watching only the final move of a chess game.

The move may be entirely visible, yet it reveals little about the reasoning that produced it. The strategy emerged through earlier positions, evaluations, alternatives, and decisions. Understanding the final move requires reconstructing the progression that made it reasonable rather than merely observing where the final piece was placed.

Computation follows a similar logic.

The significance of an intermediate representation depends not only on its content but also on how it was produced and what later processes do with it. A representation that appears minor in isolation may become essential because it redirects subsequent processing. Another may disappear quickly after performing a temporary transformation that allows later stages to proceed.

Scientific explanation therefore requires reconstructing computational processes rather than cataloging computational states.[5]

The central questions become:

How is information transformed from one stage to the next?

Which interactions preserve information, and which reorganize it?

Which sequences remain stable across different problems?

Which stages determine the direction of the processing that follows?

These questions seek to explain how coordinated interactions produce computation.

Observation reveals what exists inside a learned system.

Understanding explains how those elements become an intelligent process.

7.3 From Components to Computation

Scientific understanding develops by connecting different levels of organization rather than studying each level independently.[6]

A **component** may reveal what information is present within the system.

An **interaction** reveals how that information is exchanged, modified, strengthened, or suppressed.

A **computation** explains how successive transformations produce an intermediate result.

A **capability** emerges when many computations operate together as an organized whole.

Each level answers a different question.

A component asks:

What exists inside the system?

An interaction asks:

How do the components influence one another?

A computation asks:

How does information change as processing unfolds?

A capability asks:

How do many computations combine to produce intelligent behavior?

Scientific explanation depends on connecting these levels into one coherent account.

A representation becomes meaningful through the interactions in which it participates. Those interactions become meaningful because they contribute to an organized computation. Individual computations become scientifically significant because they help produce larger capabilities.

An explanation emerges when the causal relationships among these levels become clear.

Consider a relay race.

Knowing the abilities of every runner does not explain the team's performance. The result also depends on the order of the runners, the timing of each handoff, the speed preserved or lost during transitions, and the way one stage establishes the conditions for the next.

The explanation lies neither in the runners alone nor in the final time alone.

It lies in the organized process connecting them.

The same standard applies to artificial intelligence.

A successful explanation should not merely identify where information appears. It should show how information is progressively transformed, why particular interactions occur, how multiple computations become coordinated, and how that organization produces a capability.

Completeness therefore depends on integration rather than accumulation.

The objective is not simply to produce increasingly detailed descriptions of learned systems.

It is to explain how organized computation emerges from organized interaction.[7]

The internal organization of learned systems is increasingly visible. The remaining challenge is to connect components, interactions, computations, and capabilities within a coherent scientific account.

Seeing the parts of intelligence is an achievement.

Understanding how those parts become an intelligent process is the task that follows.

ENDNOTES

1. Mechanistic interpretability can identify internal representations, activations, components, and pathways associated with model behavior, but identifying such elements does not by itself provide a complete mechanistic explanation. Explanation additionally requires determining how the observed elements interact, what causal roles they play, and how their coordinated activity contributes to the computation being investigated.

2. In distributed computational systems, the function of a component often depends on its relationships with other components and on the larger computational context in which it participates. The same internal element may contribute differently when surrounding representations, pathways, inputs, or system states change.

3. Mechanistic explanation therefore concerns interactions as well as components. Cooperation, competition, inhibition, amplification, information routing, and alternative pathways can determine how an internal representation influences later computation. A component's function cannot always be inferred from its isolated activity or properties.

4. Neural-network computation unfolds through successive transformations of internal states. Information represented at one stage can be modified, combined, redirected, suppressed, or used to influence later processing. The functional significance of an intermediate state therefore depends partly on the computational sequence in which it occurs.

5. A mechanistic explanation aims to reconstruct the process through which internal states and transformations contribute to an outcome. Static observations can identify where particular information or activity appears, but explaining a computation requires relating those observations across causal and temporal structure.

6. Scientific explanations of complex systems often connect multiple levels of organization. For learned artificial systems, components can participate in interactions, interactions can form computations, and multiple computations can contribute to larger capabilities. Evidence at one level does not automatically explain the relationships operating at the others.

7. The standard developed in this chapter—moving from identifiable components toward an integrated account of interactions, computations, and capabilities—is part of the conceptual framework proposed in this book. It treats interpretability findings as evidence that becomes scientifically explanatory when those findings are connected into a coherent account of organized computation.

PART III

The Artificial Patient

A model's developmental history can be reconstructed. Its present computation can be examined. Its behavioral irregularities can be described as symptoms rather than conclusions. Competing mechanisms can be tested against evidence until some explanations weaken and another becomes more credible.

These are not separate forms of analysis.

Together, they constitute a way of investigating the condition of a particular learned system.

Artificial intelligence has usually been approached as something to build, optimize, evaluate, and correct. Those tasks remain essential. But once training produces a complex internal organization, a different question becomes possible.

What mechanism is operating in this system, producing this behavior, under these conditions?

A conventional software failure often suggests a bug: an incorrect instruction, a missing rule, or a defective component that can be located and repaired. A learned system may instead fail through distributed, competing, or context-dependent processes. The output may reveal that something happened without identifying where the process changed or why.

The Artificial Patient is a learned system approached through its developmental history, present organization, observable symptoms, and competing mechanistic explanations.

History reconstructs how the system became organized. It connects architecture, training, tuning, deployment, and later adaptation to the mechanisms they produced, strengthened, redirected, or preserved.

Examination asks how that organization functions now. It determines what information is represented, which processes become active, how they interact, what matters causally, and whether the same organization persists when conditions change.

Behavior appears through symptoms. A fabricated answer, inconsistent judgment, instruction failure, unstable plan, or unexpected capability identifies an event that requires interpretation. The symptom defines the problem without deciding its cause.

Differential diagnosis compares the mechanisms that could account for the evidence. Each candidate explanation generates predictions. New observations and interventions progressively weaken some possibilities while increasing support for others. The result is not a permanent label, but a working account of the mechanism most consistent with the available evidence.

This way of thinking changes what counts as successful correction.

Eliminating an unwanted response may repair the process that produced it. It may also suppress the response, redirect the output, or recruit another pathway while leaving the original tendency intact. A model may behave correctly because its internal organization has become more reliable, or because compensation temporarily preserves performance despite an unresolved weakness.

Diagnosis is what separates these possibilities.

It connects what the system has become with what it is doing now. It turns behavioral events into structured evidence and internal observations into competing explanations. It asks not merely whether the model succeeded or failed, but which internal organization made that outcome possible.

The machine has already been built.

The diagnostic task begins when we ask what kind of system learning has produced.

Limits of the Medical Analogy

The language of the Artificial Patient is methodological rather than literal. Diagnosis, prognosis, treatment, and related clinical terms provide a structure for investigating a learned system; they do not make that system a biological or human patient.

Within this framework, **diagnosis** means identifying the mechanistic explanation that best accounts for the available evidence. A **condition** refers to the organization in which a learned system currently operates—the arrangement of representations, pathways, competing processes, dependencies, and other mechanisms that shape its behavior. A condition need not represent disease, dysfunction, or pathology. A system performing successfully may still occupy a scientifically meaningful condition whose stability and future trajectory can be investigated.

Likewise, **treatment** refers to intervention on the system. It may involve altering a representation, pathway, component, training condition, or another aspect of organization and then determining what changed as a result. The clinical vocabulary is useful because it connects observation, explanation, prediction, intervention, and follow-up within a continuous investigation. Its purpose is to organize scientific reasoning, not to claim biological equivalence.

Nothing in the Artificial Patient framework requires or implies consciousness, sentience, subjective experience, suffering, personhood, or moral patienthood. Those are separate questions. The framework applies to learned artificial systems because their behavior can be investigated in relation to developmental history, internal organization, causal mechanism, intervention, and change over time—not because they are assumed to possess human or biological properties.

The analogy should therefore be judged by what it enables scientifically. Where diagnostic language helps distinguish symptoms from mechanisms, prognosis generates testable predictions, and intervention reveals whether an underlying organization changed, **the framework has scientific value**. Where the analogy ceases to improve investigation, it should not be extended.

CHAPTER 8

The Logic of Scientific Investigation

8.1 Evidence Requires Assessment

Internal observation is now possible.

Researchers can identify representations, trace portions of computational pathways, record activation patterns, alter selected components, and compare how a model responds under different conditions.

The unresolved problem is how those findings should be weighed.

An observation may be accurate without being decisive.

A feature may become active during a task, yet its activity may be incidental. A circuit may appear causally important under one prompt but contribute little when the same problem is expressed differently. An intervention may change the model's output while also disturbing several unrelated processes. A pattern may recur reliably while still admitting more than one explanation.

Scientific reasoning therefore requires a stage between observation and explanation.

That stage is **assessment**.

Observation asks:

What was found?

Assessment asks:

What does this finding support?

Evidence differs in strength, scope, and meaning.[1]

Suppose researchers identify an internal representation associated with a particular concept. The finding may recur across many prompts, but reproducibility alone does not establish that the representation produces the relevant behavior. It may accompany a broader process occurring elsewhere in the system.

Intervention provides stronger evidence.[2]

If suppressing the representation alters the model's response, the representation probably contributes causally to the computation. Yet even this result must be weighed carefully. The intervention may have disrupted several related representations, changed the balance of competing pathways, or affected later stages indirectly.

The result supports a causal role.

It does not yet define that role completely.

Assessment therefore asks several questions.

How reliably does the observation recur?

Does it appear across many examples or only under narrow conditions?

Does changing the component alter the behavior?

Is the effect specific, or does the intervention disturb several capabilities at once?

Does another method support the same conclusion?

Could the finding be explained by another mechanism?

These questions determine what the evidence can reasonably establish.

A single observation may be suggestive.

Repeated observations may make the finding more reliable.

A targeted intervention may demonstrate causal participation.

Converging evidence from several methods may support a stronger conclusion.[3]

Contradictory evidence may narrow the conditions under which the conclusion remains valid.

Assessment also defines the scope of a finding.

A mechanism may be important for one type of prompt but irrelevant to another. It may operate only when the model encounters ambiguity, unfamiliar combinations, or competing information. It may appear stable during ordinary processing but become replaceable when another pathway is available.

A scientific conclusion should match the conditions under which the evidence was obtained.[4]

If a feature contributes only during one task, the evidence supports a task-specific role.

If the same role appears across many contexts, the conclusion can be broader.

If an intervention produces different effects under different conditions, the variation is part of the finding rather than an inconvenience to be averaged away.

Assessment prevents a narrow observation from becoming an overly general claim.

It also distinguishes confidence from certainty.

Scientific evidence rarely eliminates every alternative at once. A finding may strongly support one conclusion while leaving other possibilities open. The relevant question is not whether all uncertainty has disappeared, but how much confidence the evidence justifies.

A useful assessment may therefore conclude that a mechanism is:

- reliably associated with a process;
- causally involved under defined conditions;
- necessary for one computation but replaceable in another;
- stable across several contexts;
- sensitive to surrounding activity;
- incompletely understood;
- or compatible with multiple explanations.

These are not weaknesses in scientific reasoning.

They are disciplined statements about what the evidence can and cannot support.

Assessment determines the evidential meaning of individual findings. It identifies which observations are reliable, which are causal, which are context-dependent, and which remain ambiguous.

8.2 From Findings to Competing Explanations

A learned system often produces many findings simultaneously. Some converge, some remain tentative, and some support competing mechanisms.

Scientific reasoning must determine whether those findings describe one underlying process or several processes operating together.

An explanation does more than summarize observations.

It organizes them.[5]

Suppose a model consistently produces an incorrect factual answer.

Researchers observe that the correct information exists within the model. The relevant representation becomes active during processing. A competing representation also becomes active. Strengthening the correct representation improves performance, while weakening the competing representation produces a similar improvement.

Several mechanistic accounts fit the early evidence.

The correct representation may be too weak to influence later computation.

A competing representation may dominate the decision process.

The interaction between the two representations may become unstable under particular conditions.

Later stages of computation may distort otherwise accurate intermediate results.

Each account explains part of the pattern.

The scientific task is to determine which one explains the greatest proportion of reliable evidence while remaining consistent with the findings as a whole.

Scientific reasoning therefore compares mechanisms rather than isolated observations.[6]

An explanation gains strength when independent findings converge on the same underlying process. It weakens when new evidence requires increasingly complicated assumptions to preserve it or when it cannot account for reproducible results that another explanation accommodates naturally.

The goal is not to defend the first plausible interpretation.

It is to identify the mechanism most consistent with the available evidence.

No single observation is expected to explain the system by itself.

Some findings establish that a mechanism exists.

Others determine where it operates.

Others define the conditions under which it remains active.

Still others distinguish one proposed mechanism from another.

Scientific explanation emerges from the way these findings constrain one another.

Because learned systems are highly organized, alternative mechanisms may remain viable during the early stages of investigation.

An observed failure may result from incomplete representation, unstable retrieval, competition between pathways, ineffective information integration, or distortion during later computation. Similar behavior can therefore support several mechanistic hypotheses before enough evidence has been gathered to discriminate among them.

Additional evidence progressively narrows the field.

Researchers may examine how the process behaves under different prompts, whether the same pattern appears in independently trained models, whether targeted interventions alter the result predictably, or whether comparable observations emerge during related tasks.

Each new finding changes the relative support for the alternatives.

Some hypotheses become more plausible.

Others become increasingly difficult to reconcile with the evidence.

At every stage, the explanation remains accountable to the evidence.

If new observations contradict the proposed mechanism, the explanation must be revised.[7]

If another hypothesis accounts for the findings more completely and with fewer assumptions, scientific reasoning favors the stronger account.

An explanation is therefore not a description of what was observed.

It is an evidence-based account of how the observations are causally related.

This also explains why scientific disagreement often persists after important discoveries.

Researchers may accept the same observations while proposing different mechanisms to explain them. Their disagreement concerns the organization that best accounts for the evidence.

A stable explanation begins to emerge only when the available evidence consistently favors one mechanism over its competitors.

Assessment evaluates individual findings.

Explanation integrates them into one or more causal accounts.

The remaining task is to determine which account best identifies the process operating in the particular system under investigation.

8.3 When Explanation Becomes Diagnosis

Chapter 4 established that similar outcomes can conceal different internal processes. Diagnosis is the discipline built to resolve that ambiguity.

Consider two aircraft that complete the same flight successfully.

Both depart on schedule.

Both remain stable throughout the journey.

Both land safely.

Viewed only from the outside, the two flights appear equally successful.

During routine inspection, however, engineers discover that one aircraft generated intermittent hydraulic-pressure warnings shortly before landing.

The aircraft remained controllable.

No visible malfunction occurred.

The passengers experienced a normal flight.

The warning raises an immediate question:

What produced it?

The early evidence supports multiple hypotheses.

A faulty pressure sensor may have generated a false signal.

A temporary hydraulic fluctuation may have resolved without consequence.

A control valve may have begun to fail intermittently.

A small leak may have reduced pressure while another hydraulic pathway compensated for the loss.

The successful landing cannot distinguish among these possibilities.

Additional evidence changes the picture.

Repeated testing reproduces the warning under specific operating conditions.

Inspection shows no defect in the pressure sensor.

Hydraulic-fluid levels decline slowly across successive flights.

Pressure measurements reveal increasing instability within one hydraulic circuit while neighboring systems compensate automatically to preserve normal aircraft control.

The observations now converge on a single mechanistic account.

The aircraft landed safely not because every internal system functioned normally, but because compensatory mechanisms temporarily preserved overall performance despite an emerging hydraulic fault.

The outward result concealed the process beneath it.

Several explanations were initially reasonable.

Further evidence eliminated less consistent alternatives until one mechanism provided the strongest account of the complete pattern.

Observation established what happened.

Assessment determined what each finding supported.

Explanation constructed and compared causal accounts.

The remaining task was to identify which account best described the condition of this particular aircraft.

That process is **diagnosis**.

Diagnosis is the disciplined identification of the internal mechanism most consistent with the available evidence.[8]

Explanation constructs and compares causal accounts. Diagnosis commits, provisionally, to the account that best explains the evidence in a particular system under investigation.

It does not begin with labels.

It does not assume certainty.

It does not depend on a single observation.

It weighs converging evidence, compares alternatives, eliminates less consistent accounts, and identifies the mechanism that best explains the observed condition.

The conclusion remains open to revision if new evidence appears.

The same logic applies to learned artificial intelligence systems.

A model may produce an incorrect answer.

The relevant information may never have been represented.

It may have been represented but retrieved unreliably.

Competing representations may have redirected computation.

Later processing may have distorted an otherwise correct intermediate result.

Each possibility predicts a different pattern of evidence.

Scientific investigation compares those predictions with observations gathered through replication, intervention, and internal analysis. The strongest account is the one that explains the full pattern more completely than its alternatives.

The objective is not simply to describe what the model did.

It is to determine why it did so.

A wrong answer is an observation.

The presence of relevant knowledge, the activation of competing representations, and the response to intervention are pieces of evidence.

A retrieval failure, representational conflict, or unstable computation is a possible explanation.

Diagnosis identifies which mechanistic account best fits the evidence in the model being examined.

For learned artificial intelligence, this is more than another analytical technique.

It provides a disciplined logic through which observations can be assessed, causal accounts can be compared, and conclusions about internal mechanisms can be reached without confusing outward behavior with its underlying cause.

Scientific investigation becomes diagnostic when it moves from asking what occurred to identifying the internal process that most plausibly produced it.

ENDNOTES

1. Scientific evidence differs in what it can establish. Observational association, reproducibility, causal perturbation, contextual stability, and convergence across methods support different strengths and scopes of inference. A scientifically justified claim should therefore reflect both the quality of the evidence and the conditions under which it was obtained.

2. Experimental intervention can provide stronger evidence of causal involvement than passive observation because it tests whether altering a component or process changes the outcome. Such interventions nevertheless require careful interpretation, since an alteration may affect multiple interacting components or produce indirect downstream consequences.

3. Converging evidence refers to support for a conclusion obtained through multiple observations, experimental manipulations, analytical approaches, or conditions. Agreement across partly independent sources of evidence generally strengthens a mechanistic claim because the conclusion is less dependent on the assumptions or limitations of any single method.

4. Causal and mechanistic conclusions are ordinarily conditional on the experimental context in which they were established. A component may be necessary in one task yet dispensable in another, or an alternative pathway may preserve function under particular conditions. Scientific claims should therefore specify the scope within which the evidence supports them.

5. Scientific explanation goes beyond describing observations by organizing them into accounts of the processes and causal relationships that produce the observed phenomenon. In mechanistic explanation, individual findings become informative through the way they constrain and support an account of how interacting components generate an outcome.

6. Competing-hypothesis reasoning compares alternative explanations by asking what evidence each explanation predicts and then seeking observations or interventions that discriminate among them. Evidence gains particular value when plausible alternatives make different predictions, allowing some explanations to be weakened or excluded while others receive stronger support.

7. Scientific explanations remain open to revision when new evidence conflicts with their predictions or when another account explains the observations more completely.

Provisionality is therefore not a weakness of explanation but a feature of evidence-based scientific reasoning.

8. The application of diagnostic reasoning to learned artificial systems is a conceptual extension developed in this book. The proposed framework treats diagnosis not as a medical label, but as the provisional identification of the mechanistic account that best explains the available evidence in a particular learned system after competing alternatives have been assessed and experimentally discriminated.

CHAPTER 9

Taking an Artificial History

9.1 Every Diagnosis Begins with History

A diagnosis concerns the mechanism operating in a particular system.

History asks how that mechanism came to exist.

The distinction matters because present organization is never detached from the events that produced it. A mechanism may have emerged during early training, strengthened through repeated exposure, been redirected by later tuning, or survived because another process was suppressed. Its current role reflects not only what is present now, but how the system arrived at its present state.[1]

Chapter 6 established that history can be investigated experimentally. The remaining question is what, specifically, such an investigation should reconstruct.

An artificial history is the sequence of developmental events that produced the present internal organization of a learned system.[2]

It is not simply a record of technical procedures.

A list stating that a model underwent pretraining, instruction tuning, preference optimization, and deployment may describe what engineers did. It does not yet reveal what those stages changed inside the model.

A scientifically useful history must connect each developmental event to its organizational consequences.

What representations emerged?

Which associations became dominant?

What capabilities stabilized?

Which earlier strategies were weakened, redirected, or preserved beneath later behavior?

Did a new training stage create a mechanism, modify an existing one, or merely change the conditions under which it became visible?

These questions turn a training record into a developmental account.

Consider two forests that now appear similar.

Both contain mature trees, dense vegetation, and comparable numbers of species. From a distance, their present structures may seem nearly identical.

One forest developed continuously over centuries.

The other grew after a severe wildfire, followed by deliberate replanting, invasive-species control, soil restoration, and repeated human intervention.

Their present appearances do not reveal those histories.

The first forest may contain deeply established ecological relationships that developed gradually. The second may depend on recently constructed balances, active maintenance, or combinations of species that remain vulnerable to changing conditions. A drought, new disease, or interruption of management may affect the two forests differently despite their current similarity.

History does not directly explain every process operating in either forest.

It explains why those processes exist in their present form.

A model's present mechanism may likewise become clearer after reconstructing the path through which it emerged, competed with alternatives, adapted to later objectives, and became integrated into the wider system.

The relevant history concerns development rather than chronology alone.

Chronology is insufficient; the central question is what lasting organizational change each event produced.

9.2 Initial Conditions Shape the Developmental Field

An artificial history begins before the model acquires recognizable capabilities.

The initial architecture determines how information can move, which components can interact, how signals can be combined, and what forms of organization are possible. Initialization establishes the configuration from which learning begins. The objective defines which errors matter during training. Tokenization or other input representations determine how the environment is divided into units the model can process.

These choices do not specify the final mechanism.

They shape the developmental field within which mechanisms can emerge.[3]

Two systems exposed to similar data may develop differently because their architectures provide different routes for organizing information. One structure may favor local transformations, while another supports longer-range integration. One may make certain dependencies easier to represent, while another requires those relationships to be distributed across more components.

Capacity also changes what learning can preserve.

A smaller system may compress several functions into overlapping representations because it lacks the resources to separate them. A larger system may develop more specialized pathways, retain rarer patterns, or support several strategies for the same task.[4]

The difference is not simply that one model knows more.

The organization of what it knows may be different.

The learning objective also leaves developmental consequences.

A system trained primarily to predict the next element in a sequence receives a different pattern of pressure from one trained to classify, plan, act, or optimize reward over extended interactions. The objective determines which distinctions repeatedly influence success and therefore which internal relationships are likely to strengthen.

The representation of input matters as well.

A model does not encounter raw language, images, or actions in the abstract. It encounters information divided and encoded through a particular interface. Frequently co-occurring elements may be presented as unified units, while other relationships must be reconstructed across several steps. These constraints can influence which features emerge easily and which require more distributed computation.

An artificial history should therefore ask how the model's initial conditions shaped the range of mechanisms that later became available.

The question is not merely:

Which architecture was used?

It is:

What kinds of organization did that architecture make easier, harder, or more likely to emerge?

The same reasoning applies to every early design choice.

Initialization matters when it influences which developmental path the system follows.

Capacity matters when it changes whether functions are separated, compressed, or shared.

The objective matters when it determines which strategies repeatedly receive reinforcement.

Input representation matters when it alters the basic units from which knowledge is constructed.

Initial conditions do not dictate the mature system.

They establish the landscape through which learning proceeds.

9.3 Primary Learning Creates the Foundational Organization

Pretraining or other large-scale learning stages produce the model's first extensive internal organization.

During this period, the system encounters recurring patterns, adjusts its parameters, develops representations, and establishes relationships that later learning will inherit.

This stage is not simply the acquisition of information.

It is the construction of a foundation upon which later capabilities depend.

A representation that emerges early may influence how subsequent information is interpreted. A frequently reinforced association may become the default route through which related inputs are processed. A useful shortcut may stabilize before a more general strategy has enough evidence to form. Once established, these patterns can shape what later learning can easily preserve or modify.

The content of the training environment matters through the organization it repeatedly rewards.

Frequency affects which patterns become dominant.

Diversity affects whether representations generalize across contexts or remain tied to narrow regularities.

Ordering can influence which distinctions become established before others.

Curriculum can determine whether complex capabilities are built upon stable simpler mechanisms or assembled through less reliable alternatives.[5]

Optimization also contributes to developmental history.

The route taken through the parameter space is not merely a technical detail. It determines which among many possible internal solutions becomes embedded in the model. Different random seeds, data orders, learning rates, or optimization schedules may produce systems with similar performance but distinct internal arrangements.[6]

An artificial history should therefore ask which mechanisms appeared first, which remained stable, which were replaced, and which became increasingly integrated with other capabilities.

The timing of emergence can be diagnostically important.

A mechanism acquired early may become deeply embedded because later representations develop around it. Altering it may affect many capabilities that now depend on the same foundation.

A mechanism acquired later may remain more localized or weakly integrated. It may be easier to modify without disrupting the rest of the system.

Two mechanisms that perform the same visible function may therefore carry different diagnostic implications depending on when and how they emerged.

History also reveals whether a mature capability developed gradually or appeared after a sharp reorganization.

Gradual development may indicate that many small changes progressively refined an existing process. Abrupt emergence may indicate that previously separate representations reached a point at which they could interact in a new way.

The resulting capability may appear similar in either case, while resting on a different developmental basis.

9.4 Later Tuning Reorganizes What Already Exists

Later training does not begin with an empty system.

Instruction tuning, preference optimization, reinforcement, safety training, and domain-specific adaptation act upon an organization that has already been formed.[7]

Their effects cannot be understood as independent additions.

A later stage may strengthen an existing pathway, suppress it through competition, or redirect how its information reaches the output. It may also introduce new associations that become entangled with older ones. Its developmental meaning therefore depends on what was present before it began.

Suppose a model already contains a strong association that frequently produces an undesirable response. Later training discourages that response until it becomes rare.

Several organizational outcomes are possible.

The original association may have weakened.

A competing representation may now suppress it.

The output-selection process may have been redirected while the earlier computation remains intact.

The triggering conditions may have narrowed.

The model may have learned a second strategy that dominates in familiar evaluation settings but fails under unusual prompts.

The reduction in the response does not reveal which of these changes occurred.

A useful artificial history must therefore distinguish behavioral change from organizational change.

What did the later training actually modify?

Did it create a new mechanism?

Did it alter the influence of an old one?

Did it change only the final stage of response selection?

Did it reorganize several shared representations?

Did it preserve an earlier tendency in a latent form?

These are historical questions because their answers require comparison across developmental stages.

A final model examined alone may show only the present balance among competing mechanisms. Earlier checkpoints may reveal that one process previously dominated, another emerged later, and the current behavior reflects an unstable compromise between them.[8]

Later tuning can also create dependencies that were absent during primary learning.

A preference-optimized model may become more sensitive to particular contextual signals because those signals repeatedly indicated which responses received approval. A safety-tuned system may develop pathways that monitor for particular topics or instructions. Domain adaptation may strengthen specialized representations while weakening broader performance through competition for shared resources.

Some changes become deeply integrated.

Others remain narrow and conditional.

Some preserve earlier organization while altering its expression.

Others replace the route through which a capability is produced.

An artificial history records these consequences rather than merely naming the procedure that caused them.

9.5 Deployment Can Continue Development

Training does not always end when the model is released.

A deployed system may receive new information through memory, retrieval, tools, external databases, user-specific adaptation, or continued fine-tuning. Its outputs may depend on resources that did not exist during pretraining. Its effective organization may therefore extend beyond the fixed parameters of the base model.

This later experience belongs in the history whenever it changes how the system processes information.

Memory may allow earlier interactions to influence later responses. Retrieval may introduce external information that competes with or overrides internal knowledge. Tool use may shift part of a task from internal reasoning to external execution. Continued adaptation may strengthen specialized habits in response to a narrow deployment environment.

Even without permanent parameter updates, the functioning system may change.[9]

The history of a deployed system therefore includes changes to its surrounding cognitive environment as well as changes to the model itself.

Two deployments may use the same base model while functioning as different systems.

One may have access to reliable retrieval, stable memory, and carefully constrained tools.

Another may operate with incomplete databases, conflicting memories, or tools that produce noisy results.

The underlying parameters are identical.

The functioning systems are not.

An artificial history must identify which parts of present behavior arise from the learned model, which arise from later additions, and how those elements interact.

Otherwise, a mechanism may be attributed to the model when it actually depends on retrieval. A failure may be blamed on internal knowledge when the relevant external information was never supplied. A capability may appear to have emerged through training when it is produced by a newly available tool.

Developmental context clarifies the boundaries of the system being diagnosed.

9.6 History Narrows Diagnosis

History does not replace examination of the present model.

It changes how present evidence is interpreted.

The ambiguity established in Chapter 4 becomes narrower once developmental history is available: similar behavior may conceal not only different mechanisms, but mechanisms formed at different stages and integrated to different depths.

Suppose two systems produce the same unusual response.

One developed the underlying association during pretraining and retained it through every later stage. The other acquired a similar response only after narrow domain adaptation.

In the first system, the association may be deeply integrated with broad representations and shared across many tasks. In the second, it may depend on a localized later pathway that activates only within a particular context.

The diagnostic investigation should proceed differently.

A foundational mechanism may require tracing dependencies across several capabilities, whereas a later specialized mechanism may be localized to a narrower developmental stage.

History narrows the plausible explanations before intervention begins.

It can reveal whether a current behavior is likely to reflect:

- a foundational representation established early;
- a shortcut rewarded by a particular training environment;
- a later mechanism layered over an older one;
- a suppressed process that remains available;
- competition created by incompatible training objectives;
- or dependence on resources added during deployment.

The point is not to assign every mechanism to one isolated event.

Development is cumulative, and later organization often reflects interactions among many stages.

The resulting organization therefore carries traces of the developmental sequence that produced it, as illustrated in **Figure 4.**

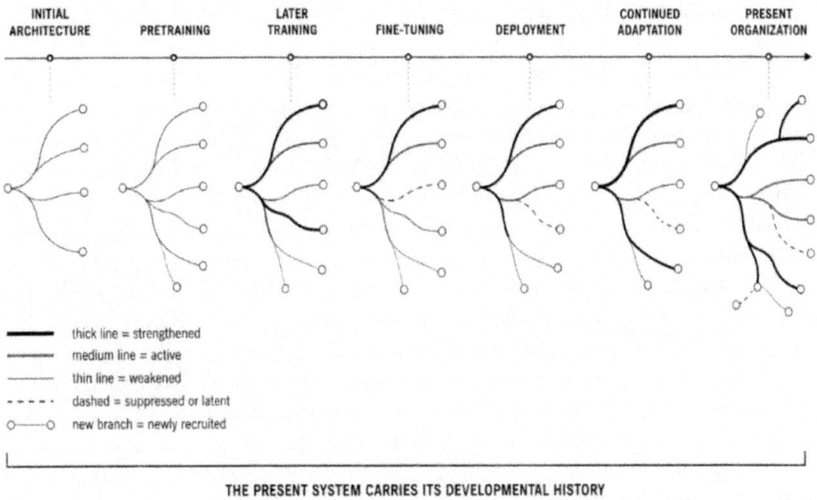

Figure 4. The Present System Carries Its Developmental History.

History identifies where the investigation should look and which developmental pathways remain plausible.

It also changes the meaning of apparent stability.

A mechanism that has survived multiple rounds of tuning may be more deeply integrated than one that appeared recently. A behavior that disappears after fine-tuning may still recur if the older pathway remains intact. A capability supported by several independently acquired mechanisms may resist modification because removing one route leaves another available.

Without history, these possibilities can look like unexplained variation.

With history, they become testable hypotheses.

Failed interventions provide another use for developmental history.

An attempted correction may target the mechanism visible in the final model while leaving untouched an earlier process that can reassert itself under different conditions. Another intervention may appear broadly disruptive because it modifies a foundational representation upon which many later capabilities were built.

That is why history belongs at the beginning of diagnosis.

A present-day examination can reveal what organization is operating now. History identifies the changes that made that organization possible.

Diagnosis asks:

What mechanism best explains the current evidence?

Artificial history adds the question that must follow:

How did this system become organized so that this mechanism could exist?

ENDNOTES

1. Learned systems can exhibit path dependence: their present organization may reflect not only the information available now but also the sequence of training, optimization, fine-tuning, and later adaptation through which that organization developed. Earlier learning can constrain, facilitate, or alter the effects of later learning.

2. *Artificial history*, as used in this book, is a proposed component of the Artificial Patient framework. It extends the ordinary record of model architecture and training procedures into a developmental investigation of how successive learning events contributed to the internal organization observed in the present system.

3. Neural-network architecture, parameter initialization, learning objectives, and input representations constrain the optimization problem through which a model develops. These factors do not uniquely determine the final learned mechanism, but they influence the structures, representations, and computational solutions that are available or comparatively easy for optimization to discover.

4. Model capacity can influence not only how much information a system can represent but also how that information and computation are internally organized. Limited capacity may encourage greater sharing or compression of representational resources, while increased capacity can permit more differentiated, specialized, or redundant internal solutions.

5. Learning can depend on the order and structure of experience. Data ordering and curriculum design may alter which representations or strategies become established early and thereby influence how subsequent information is learned. The resulting system can therefore reflect the trajectory of learning rather than only the final collection of examples encountered.

6. Neural-network optimization can converge on different internal solutions across training runs even when architecture, task, and overall performance are similar. Random initialization, minibatch or data order, optimization hyperparameters, and other training contingencies can influence which among multiple functionally adequate solutions becomes embedded in a trained system.

7. Post-training procedures such as instruction tuning, preference optimization, reinforcement-based training, safety tuning, and domain adaptation modify a model whose representations and computational pathways were already shaped by earlier learning. Their effects can therefore include reinforcement, suppression, redirection, or reorganization of existing mechanisms rather than simply the addition of isolated new capabilities.

8. Comparing model checkpoints across training or fine-tuning provides a longitudinal way to investigate when representations, pathways, or behaviors emerge and how their roles change. Such comparisons can help distinguish mechanisms established early in development from those introduced, strengthened, suppressed, or reorganized during later stages.

9. The behavior of a deployed AI system can depend on more than the fixed parameters of its base model. Retrieval systems, external memory, tools, databases, context, and continued adaptation can alter the information available to computation and the pathways through which tasks are completed. Two deployments using the same underlying model can therefore function differently because their surrounding computational environments differ.

CHAPTER 10

Examining the Machine Mind

A learned system may contain far more information than it uses to produce a particular response. Some representations remain inactive, others compete for influence, and still others become relevant only under particular conditions. Two identical outputs may therefore arise from different internal organizations, while different outputs may diverge only late in an otherwise similar computation.

Examination begins with the computation itself: which parts of the learned organization participated in producing this response?

Suppose a model receives the instruction:

Summarize this article, but focus primarily on the experimental methods rather than the conclusions.

The resulting summary describes the conclusions extensively while giving only brief attention to the methods.

The output leaves several explanations open. The model may not have represented the user's priority correctly. It may have represented both objectives but assigned greater influence to the wrong one. The intended emphasis may have weakened during later processing, or a competing pathway may have redirected the response before generation began.

The incorrect summary does not reveal which of these possibilities occurred.

A systematic examination moves from availability to participation, from participation to transformation, and from observed organization to causal and contextual testing. Together, these forms of evidence reveal how the response emerged from the system's organization at that moment.

10.1 Examining What the System Represents

The first task is to determine whether the information required for the response exists within the model in a usable form.

A learned system develops internal representations of concepts, linguistic relationships, procedures, visual structures, and patterns acquired across training. These representations may be explicit and localized, widely distributed, or recoverable only through combinations of internal activity. Their existence cannot always be inferred from a model's immediate behavior.[1]

A model may produce an incorrect response despite possessing the information needed to answer correctly. Conversely, a correct response does not necessarily show that the relevant information exists in a stable and reusable form. The result may depend on contextual cues, overlapping associations, or a pathway that happened to reach the appropriate output under one narrow set of conditions.

The ambiguous instruction illustrates the problem. The request contains two related but separable objectives. The model must produce a summary, and it must organize that summary around the experimental methods rather than the conclusions.

An examination first asks whether both objectives were represented.

Did the system encode the general task of summarization?

Did it also encode the instruction to prioritize methodology?

If the second objective never formed as a meaningful internal representation, the later failure begins at the earliest stage of processing. The system cannot preserve a priority that was never adequately encoded.

The representation may also exist in an incomplete form. The model might register that the methods are relevant without capturing the stronger requirement that they should dominate the summary. In that case, the failure would not reflect total absence but insufficient precision. The information entered the system, yet its internal form did not preserve the relationship intended by the user.

A further possibility is that both objectives were represented accurately. The system understood that it should summarize the article and that the methods should receive primary emphasis. If so, the explanation cannot stop at comprehension. Information that exists within the system does not automatically determine how the system will behave.

Representation establishes what the model can potentially use, not what actually shaped the response[2]. The examination must therefore determine which available representations entered the computation and how strongly they participated.

10.2 Examining the Current State

A representation may exist within the model yet remain absent from the computation that produces a particular response.

Learned systems contain many more potential representations than can influence any single task. Context, wording, recent inputs, competing objectives, and the current computational state determine which portions of that larger organization become active.[3] The same model may therefore respond differently to equivalent instructions without undergoing any lasting change in its stored knowledge.

Suppose the examination shows that the model represented both parts of the instruction correctly. It encoded the request to summarize and the requirement to emphasize experimental methods. Both goals were available when processing began.

The investigation now asks which of those goals actually became engaged while the summary was being constructed.

Did the representation of the experimental methods remain active?

Did the general objective of producing a conventional summary become more prominent?

Were both goals active simultaneously?

Did one remain weak from the beginning, or did it initially participate and later fade?

These questions concern the current state of the computation. They do not ask what the model possesses in general, but what portions of its learned organization became involved under this particular set of conditions.

Two models may contain similar information while recruiting it differently. One may maintain the methodological priority throughout the task. Another may activate it only briefly before stronger learned associations with article summaries begin to dominate. The difference would not lie in whether the models understood the instruction, but in how their current states organized the available information.

The same model may also recruit different representations when the instruction is paraphrased. A request to "focus primarily on the experimental methods" may produce one internal state, while "devote most of the summary to how the study was conducted" may produce another. The underlying objective remains similar, yet the wording changes which associations and representations become active.

Measures of internal activity help identify the parts of the learned organization that entered the computation, including representations that appeared only briefly or competed without prevailing.[4] A representation that never becomes active cannot influence the response, regardless of how accurately it was acquired during development.

Participation still does not explain the outcome. Active representations may be strengthened, weakened, combined, suppressed, or redirected as processing unfolds.

10.3 Following the Computational Process

A computation is not a single event. It is a sequence of transformations through which information changes its role, influence, and relationship to other information.[5]

Suppose both goals remain active during the early stages of processing. The model represents the need to summarize the article and the need to prioritize its methods. At this point, neither success nor failure has been determined. Both objectives participate in the computation.

Their relative influence may change as the response develops.

The concept of summarization may activate strong learned associations with identifying major findings, extracting central claims, and presenting conclusions. Those associations may become increasingly influential as the model begins organizing the response. The instruction to foreground the methods may remain present, but its contribution may weaken as the more familiar summary pattern gains control.

The shift may occur early. The system may recognize both objectives during instruction processing but begin planning the answer around the conclusions almost immediately.

It may occur later. The model may initially construct a method-focused response, then redirect attention toward the findings as it integrates information from the article.

It may also arise through competition among several pathways. One pathway may preserve the user's requested emphasis, while another follows the article's semantic prominence or the model's stronger learned expectations about what summaries normally contain.

The relevant question is not merely whether both goals became active. It is how their relationship changed as the response took shape.

Similar summaries may diverge internally at very different stages of processing. In one case, the methodological priority may disappear almost immediately. In another, it may remain influential until late in the computation and lose control only when the final wording is selected. The external result may look comparable, but the point of failure would differ.

Following the computational process reveals where information is preserved, transformed, redirected, or overtaken by competing influences. It can show where an instruction loses strength, where contextual information changes its interpretation, and where one pathway begins to dominate the alternatives.

Examining the current state identifies which representations participate. Following the computational process explains how those representations interact to produce the final behavior. Participation provides a series of internal snapshots. Process analysis reconstructs the sequence through which those states become an organized response.

By this stage, the examination may have identified a plausible mechanism. The model represented both objectives, recruited both during early processing, and then allowed the general summary pathway to dominate the pathway carrying the user's requested emphasis.

The pattern is suggestive, but its repeated presence does not yet establish that it determined the outcome.

10.4 Testing Causal Involvement

Representation, activation, and pathway analysis describe the computation, but they do not establish which components determined the result. Some representations shape the response directly. Others accompany processes driven elsewhere.

A mechanism that accompanies a response is not necessarily the mechanism that generates it.[6]

The ambiguous instruction may consistently produce stronger activity associated with the article's conclusions. That pattern could reflect the cause of the misplaced emphasis. It could also be a consequence of another process that has already determined the direction of the response.

Causal testing alters a suspected component and observes whether the computation changes in the predicted way.

Suppose the representation carrying the instruction to prioritize methodology is selectively strengthened while the remaining computation is preserved as closely as possible. If the resulting summary gives substantially greater attention to the methods, the intervention supports the view that this representation contributed to the original failure. Its weakness was not merely observable; it mattered to the outcome.

If the summary remains unchanged, the explanation becomes less convincing. The methodological representation may have been too far removed from the process that determined the response, or another mechanism may have prevented it from affecting later stages.

The opposite intervention can provide complementary evidence. A representation associated with the conclusions may appear increasingly dominant as the summary develops. Weakening its influence may reveal whether that pathway was responsible for displacing the user's priority.

A large change in the response would support its causal involvement. Little or no change would suggest that the visible activity was not the principal driver, or that another pathway compensated when it was disrupted.

The same logic applies to intermediate pathways. If the methodological priority appears to weaken at a particular stage, preserving that pathway can test whether its loss caused the incorrect emphasis. Correction would support the explanation; an unchanged response would place the decisive process elsewhere.

In this examination, intervention serves to distinguish among competing mechanistic explanations rather than to optimize performance.

The results may also reveal that no single component controls the behavior. Learned systems often distribute functions across overlapping pathways. Several routes may support the same response, allowing one to compensate when another is weakened. A mechanism can therefore be causally involved without being strictly necessary under every condition.[7]

Conversely, a small intervention may produce a large effect when it targets a component positioned upstream of many later transformations. The magnitude of the altered component does not necessarily predict the magnitude of the behavioral change.

The examination therefore seeks a causal organization rather than one isolated cause. It asks how multiple representations and pathways contribute together, which mechanisms carry unique influence, which provide redundancy, and which remain incidental to the response.

For the ambiguous instruction, the resulting explanation might be more complex than a single goal overpowering another. The model may represent the methodological priority accurately, maintain it through early processing, and then lose its influence when a strongly learned summary pattern organizes the response. That later pattern may be supported by several overlapping pathways, making it resistant to changes in any one component.

Causal testing converts the observed sequence into a functional account of what mattered. The remaining question is whether that account describes a stable tendency of the system or only one route produced under one narrow set of circumstances.

10.5 Examining Stability Across Conditions

A mechanism identified in one computation may reflect a general property of the model, or it may depend on the exact wording, context, and competing information present at that moment.[8]

The instruction can therefore be varied while its underlying objective remains intact.

The model might be asked to:

Summarize the study, devoting most of the response to the experimental design and procedures.

Or:

Explain how the researchers conducted the study. Mention the findings only briefly.

The article may remain the same while the instruction becomes more explicit. The instruction may remain the same while the article changes. Additional distracting information may be introduced, the context may become longer, or the methodological details may become less prominent in the source material.

Each variation tests whether the same internal organization continues to govern the response.

If the model repeatedly represents the methodological priority, recruits it during early processing, and then allows a conventional summary pathway to dominate, the explanation gains broader force. The examination has identified an enduring tendency rather than an isolated computational event.

If the mechanism changes across paraphrases, the original explanation must be narrowed. One wording may fail because the priority representation remains weak. Another may preserve that priority but lose it during later processing. A third may produce the desired response through a different pathway altogether.

Variation does not weaken the examination. It reveals the range of organizations available to the system.

A learned model may possess several ways of solving what appears externally to be the same task. Some routes may be reliable, others fragile, and others highly dependent on specific contextual cues. Stability testing shows whether the proposed mechanism remains active, reorganizes, or disappears when those cues change.

This also prevents one successful intervention from being mistaken for a complete explanation. Strengthening a representation may correct the behavior under one phrasing but fail under another because the second condition recruits a different computational route. The first intervention may have identified a genuine mechanism while addressing only one member of a broader family.

A robust explanation should therefore account for related computations that preserve the same underlying problem while varying their superficial form. Stability determines whether the proposed mechanism reflects an enduring organizational tendency or only one context-dependent route through the system.

10.6 Building an Examination Profile

The investigation has established what information was represented, identified which representations became active, reconstructed how their influence changed, tested which components affected the outcome, and determined whether the proposed organization persisted across changing conditions.

Taken together, these observations constitute an examination profile.[9]

An examination profile is not a collection of isolated measurements. It is an integrated description of how a learned system was organized during the computation under investigation.

In the ambiguous-instruction case, the profile might show that the model encoded both goals accurately. The methodological priority became active but remained weaker than the general summarization objective. As processing unfolded, learned associations between summarization and major conclusions redirected the response. Interventions that preserved the methodological pathway improved the output, although the effect varied across alternative phrasings because some instructions recruited partially different routes.

This account reveals more than the fact that the model followed the wrong emphasis. It identifies where the intended goal entered the system, how long it remained influential, where its contribution weakened, which competing processes shaped the outcome, and how consistently the same pattern reappeared.

The profile has a focused purpose: to establish the present-state evidence required to explain a specific computation.

The examination profile establishes the present-state evidence required for diagnosis. The next question is what underlying condition best explains that organization and its observable effects.

ENDNOTES

1. Internal information can be present in a learned model without being expressed reliably in its immediate behavior. Representation-level analyses can reveal information that is recoverable from internal states even when the model does not consistently use that information to generate the observed output.

2. The presence of a representation does not establish its causal or computational role in a particular response. Distinguishing information that is available within the model from information that actually participates in a computation is an important step in mechanistic analysis.

3. Internal activity in neural networks is strongly context dependent. Changes in wording, preceding context, competing instructions, or task conditions can alter which representations and computational pathways are recruited even when the underlying task appears behaviorally similar.

4. Activation analysis, representation probing, and related interpretability methods examine internal states produced during model computation. Such measurements can identify when particular information is present or active, but observational activity alone does not establish that the measured representation causally influenced the final behavior.

5. Neural-network computation unfolds through successive transformations rather than through the static presence of information alone. Mechanistic analysis therefore often requires tracing how representations are transmitted, transformed, combined, amplified, suppressed, or redirected across stages of processing.

6. Correlation between an internal representation or component and an observed behavior does not by itself establish causal involvement. Mechanistic claims are strengthened when targeted interventions produce predicted changes in the computation or output while relevant alternative explanations are controlled.

7. Distributed learned systems may contain overlapping, redundant, or compensatory computational routes. Disrupting one component may therefore leave behavior intact because another pathway can support the same outcome. Conversely, a component may contribute causally without being individually necessary under every condition.

8. Mechanistic explanations should be tested across related conditions to determine their scope. Paraphrased instructions, altered contexts, changed inputs, added distractors, and other controlled variations can reveal whether an identified mechanism is stable across conditions or specific to one computational route.

9. *Examination profile*, as used in this book, is a proposed component of the Artificial Patient framework. It refers to an integrated present-state account combining evidence about represented information, active internal states, computational pathways, causal contributions, competing processes, and stability across conditions. Its purpose is to provide the mechanistic evidence from which a subsequent diagnosis can be constructed.

CHAPTER 11

Hallucination Is a Symptom, Not a Diagnosis

A model is asked to provide the source for a scientific claim. It responds confidently with the title of an article, the names of several authors, the name of a journal, and a publication year.

The citation appears plausible.

The article does not exist.

The behavior is commonly called a hallucination.[1]

That name identifies what appeared in the response. It does not establish why the response appeared.

The model may never have learned the relevant source. It may possess information about the source but fail to retrieve it. A familiar citation pattern may dominate weaker evidence. Correct fragments from several articles may be combined into a nonexistent reference. The system's representation of uncertainty may be too weak to interrupt generation, or it may continue producing a fluent answer after the available evidence has been exhausted.

Each mechanism can produce the same observable outcome: a confident but fabricated citation.[2]

Figure 5 makes this distinction explicit: a single outward symptom can be produced by several different internal mechanisms.

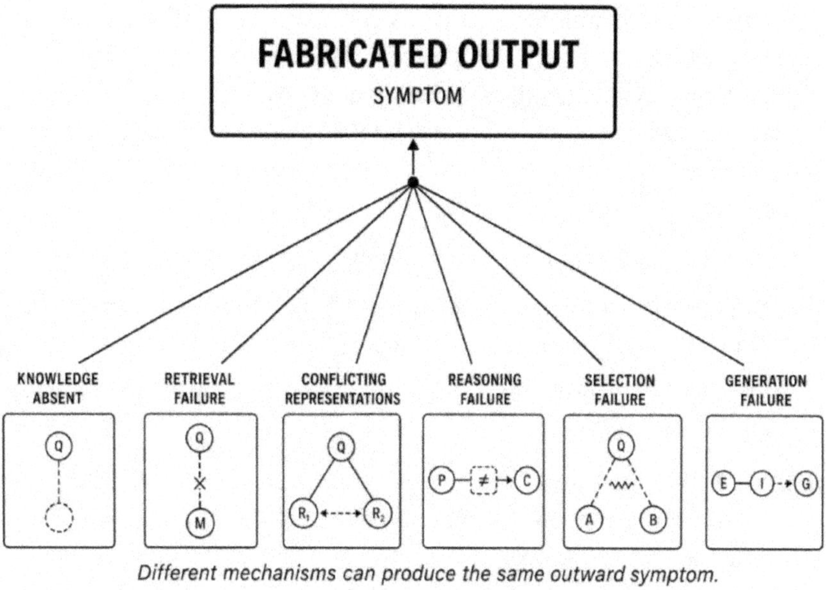

Figure 5. Different Mechanisms Can Produce the Same Symptom.

The behavior is therefore a symptom, not a diagnosis.

A symptom is a behavioral manifestation whose underlying mechanism has not yet been established.[3] It records that something occurred—a false statement, an inconsistent answer, an instruction failure, an unstable plan, or an unexpected capability. It does not identify the internal condition responsible.

Investigation begins with the behavior while leaving its cause unresolved.

Calling the fabricated citation a hallucination remains useful because the label describes the visible form of the failure. The problem begins when that behavioral category is treated as though it names a single internal condition. Failures originating in knowledge, retrieval, competition, uncertainty, integration, or generation can all receive the same label despite arising from different organizations.

11.1 Symptoms Are Observable Evidence

An observable response becomes diagnostically useful when it is described precisely.

The statement that a model "hallucinated" leaves several questions unanswered. What exactly was unsupported? Was the entire answer invented, or only one detail? Did the model fabricate a source despite having access to reliable evidence? Did the failure occur once, or recur across related requests? Did the model express uncertainty, or present the answer with complete confidence?

A more precise description of the citation failure would be:

The model confidently generated a plausible but nonexistent scientific source in response to a request for supporting evidence.

That description identifies the observable irregularity without assigning its cause.

It distinguishes the event from nearby symptoms. The model did not merely give an incomplete answer. It did not refuse the request, misformat a correct citation, or openly acknowledge uncertainty. It produced a specific source whose structure resembled a legitimate reference but whose identity could not be verified.

The conditions surrounding the behavior refine its meaning.

Does the model fabricate citations only when asked about obscure subjects?

Does the behavior persist when retrieval tools are available?

Does it occur when the underlying scientific claim is correct?

Does requesting a direct quotation reduce the failure?

Does the model repeat the same nonexistent source or generate a different one each time?

Does the answer change when the question is paraphrased?

These observations define the symptom's form, boundaries, and reproducibility.[4]

A useful symptom description records its content, context, consistency, severity, and responsiveness to changing conditions. Content identifies what changed. Context identifies when it appeared. Consistency shows whether it was isolated or recurrent. Severity records how far the response departed from the evidence. Responsiveness shows whether wording, tools, or surrounding information altered its expression.

These properties separate events that might otherwise receive the same label.

A model that invents one bibliographic detail in a long answer presents a different pattern from one that repeatedly fabricates entire references. A model that produces nonexistent sources only when no retrieval system is available differs from one that ignores valid retrieved evidence and continues generating unsupported citations. Both behaviors may be called hallucination, but their scope and conditions differ.

Precision prevents the label from becoming more explanatory than the evidence allows.

Hallucination, inconsistency, rigidity, and failure remain useful when they describe recurring forms of behavior. They become misleading when their names are treated as explanations for the processes beneath them.

A fabricated citation, a false historical claim, an unsupported scientific inference, and an answer produced from insufficient evidence may all belong to the broad category of hallucination. Their shared feature is inadequate support. Their internal origins may have little else in common.

A behavioral category can organize symptoms without defining a diagnostic condition.

11.2 One Symptom, Many Mechanisms

The same fabricated citation can arise through several internal routes.

The simplest possibility is missing knowledge. The model may never have acquired a reliable representation of the relevant source. Asked to provide one, it generates a plausible reference from patterns learned across similar citations.

Information associated with the source may instead exist within the model but fail to become available during the response. The relevant representation may remain weak, inaccessible, or displaced by more familiar associations.

Retrieval can also succeed without controlling the output.[5] A correct source may enter the computation while a stronger pattern associated with common author names, journal titles, and publication formats shapes the final citation.

The model may combine accurate fragments incorrectly. A real author from one article, the title structure of another, and the journal associated with a third may be integrated into a reference that appears coherent but has never existed.

The failure may originate in uncertainty rather than source knowledge. The system may possess only partial evidence but fail to represent that limitation strongly enough to stop, qualify, or refuse the answer.[6] Fluency then fills the space left by weak evidence.

Generation may also continue beyond the point supported by the available information. The model may begin with a valid scientific claim and then produce a citation because the structure of the response strongly predicts that one should follow, even though no verified reference is available.

The symptom alone cannot distinguish among these possibilities.

Premature labeling can direct the investigation toward the wrong process. Calling the event a knowledge failure focuses attention on what the model learned. Calling it a retrieval failure shifts attention toward access. Calling it a calibration failure emphasizes uncertainty. Calling it a generation failure directs scrutiny toward later stages of response production.

Any of these interpretations may prove correct. The fabricated reference does not choose among them.

Different proposed mechanisms imply different interventions.

Adding reliable source material may help when knowledge is missing, while stronger retrieval may help when the correct source remains inaccessible. Neither will correct a failure in which retrieved evidence is repeatedly displaced by a dominant citation pattern.

Requiring the model to abstain when confidence is low may reduce unsupported answers. It may also suppress valid responses without correcting the process that produced the fabrication.

A verification tool may prevent nonexistent citations from reaching the final output. The underlying tendency to construct plausible references may remain intact and reappear when verification is absent.

Behavioral improvement does not by itself reveal which mechanism changed.[7]

A fabricated citation may disappear without its source being repaired, and it may persist after one contributing mechanism has been altered because another pathway produces the same result. Several mechanisms can therefore converge on the same behavioral form, making symptom labels useful for organizing observations but insufficient for organizing explanations.

11.3 One Mechanism, Many Symptoms

A single mechanism can produce different symptoms under different conditions.

Suppose examination identifies a recurring organization in which a fluent-completion pathway overrides weaker evidence constraints. When the model encounters an incomplete informational state, the pressure to continue a coherent answer remains stronger than the signal that the available evidence is insufficient.

In a citation task, this mechanism may produce a plausible but nonexistent reference.

In a factual question, it may produce an unsupported claim stated with confidence.

When corrected by the user, the model may acknowledge the correction but generate another unsupported explanation because fluency again overtakes the weaker evidence constraint. The symptom now appears as resistance to correction.

The same organization may therefore appear as fabrication, overconfidence, or resistance to correction depending on the task and available evidence.[8] Conversely, behaviorally similar failures may still arise from different processes. Relationships among symptoms become mechanistically meaningful only when they recur under related conditions and respond similarly to targeted intervention.

A mechanism is defined neither by one behavior nor by a fixed inventory of symptoms. Its expression depends on where it operates, which other processes are active, and what demands the current task places on the system.

11.4 Symptoms Guide Investigation

Symptoms determine where diagnosis begins.

Once the fabricated citation has been described precisely, its conditions begin narrowing the possible mechanisms.

If the behavior appears only when no retrieval system is available, missing or inaccessible information becomes more plausible.

If the correct article is retrieved but does not shape the answer, attention shifts toward competition or integration.

If the model represents uncertainty but continues generating the citation, later response production becomes more relevant.

If abstention instructions prevent the fabrication only under narrow wording, the behavior may depend on unstable control rather than absence of uncertainty.

If the same internal pathway contributes to unsupported facts, invented sources, and resistance to correction, the investigation may be approaching a broader mechanism.

Hallucination becomes diagnostically useful only after its form, context, and recurrence have been specified.

Behavioral taxonomies organize recurring forms of output, but their boundaries need not correspond to boundaries between mechanisms. One symptom category may contain several causes, while different categories may share one.

The separation preserves the value of both. Symptoms can be recorded and compared without assuming that their causes are already known. Mechanisms can be investigated without requiring every instance to produce the same behavioral expression.

The symptom label remains useful when it is restricted to describing the observable behavior. Behaviorally similar instances may remain open to different diagnoses.

Its form defines the search. Its context narrows the possibilities. Its recurrence reveals scope. Its response to intervention changes the support for competing mechanisms.

A model may fail in one way for several reasons. One mechanism may cause the model to fail in several ways. Between those possibilities lies the central task of diagnosis: distinguishing the mechanism that best explains this symptom, in this system, under these conditions.

ENDNOTES

1. In research on large language models, *hallucination* is commonly used for generated content that is unsupported, inconsistent with available evidence, or factually incorrect despite being presented as plausible output. Definitions vary across studies, and the term generally characterizes an observable failure rather than specifying a single underlying computational mechanism.

2. Similar language-model failures can arise from different stages or components of processing, including limitations in stored information, retrieval, contextual integration, uncertainty handling, selection among competing representations, and generation. The use of these alternatives as competing mechanistic diagnoses is part of the investigative framework developed in this book.

3. *Symptom*, as used in the Artificial Patient framework, is a proposed methodological term for an observable behavioral manifestation whose underlying mechanism remains unresolved. It deliberately separates description of what the system did from explanation of why the system did it.

4. Language-model behavior can vary substantially with prompt wording, context, available tools, retrieved evidence, sampling conditions, and repeated trials. Evaluating a failure across related conditions therefore helps establish its reproducibility, boundaries, and dependence on contextual factors rather than treating a single output as a complete characterization of the system.

5. Providing or retrieving relevant information does not guarantee that a language model will use that information faithfully in producing its answer. Retrieved evidence must still influence later computation and generation, and models may ignore, underweight, misintegrate, or override relevant context. Retrieval success and successful use of retrieved information are therefore distinct questions.

6. Confidence expressed in generated language need not correspond reliably to the strength of the model's underlying evidence. Research on calibration, uncertainty estimation, selective prediction, and abstention examines whether systems can appropriately represent uncertainty and refrain from answering when available evidence is insufficient.

7. A successful behavioral intervention does not by itself identify the internal change responsible for the improved output. Editing, prompting, retrieval, filtering, verification, or control mechanisms may repair an underlying process, suppress its expression, bypass it, or compensate through another route. Distinguishing these possibilities requires mechanistic examination after intervention.

8. The symptom–mechanism relationship proposed in this book is many-to-many. Behaviorally similar failures may arise from different internal processes, while the same underlying organization may produce different outward failures as task demands and contextual conditions change. This principle provides the basis for treating behavioral categories as starting points for mechanistic diagnosis rather than as diagnoses themselves.

CHAPTER 12

Differential Diagnosis

A model is given three statements:

Every Luma is a Ven.
No Ven is a Rel.
Can anything be both a Luma and a Rel?

The model answers correctly:

No. If every Luma is a Ven and no Ven is a Rel, then no Luma can be a Rel.

The same problem is then expressed differently:

All objects classified as Lumas belong to the category of Vens. Vens and Rels never overlap. Is it possible for an object to belong to both the Luma and Rel categories?

The model answers:

Yes, an object could potentially belong to both categories because classification systems may overlap.

The two questions express the same logical relationship. The model reaches opposite conclusions.

The contradiction is the symptom.

Several diagnostic hypotheses remain possible.

The model may not have represented the logical structure consistently across the two phrasings. It may have encoded the premises correctly but relied on different reasoning pathways. A surface association triggered by words such as "categories" and "overlap" may have competed with the formal relationship. The correct conclusion may have formed internally but failed to control the final answer. The contradiction may also reflect instability during generation rather than reasoning itself.

Each explanation is compatible with the visible behavior.

Differential diagnosis begins when plausible explanations are treated as competing hypotheses rather than interchangeable descriptions.[1]

A **diagnostic hypothesis** is a proposed mechanism that could account for the available evidence. Its value depends not merely on whether it can explain what has already happened, but on whether it generates expectations about what should happen under new conditions.[2]

Those expectations are **diagnostic predictions**.

A model that failed to represent the premises should behave differently from one that represented them correctly but followed a misleading surface cue. A model with unstable reasoning should respond differently from one whose internal conclusion is stable but whose final answer selection is unreliable.

The hypotheses may fit the original contradiction equally well.

Their predictions do not.

12.1 Competing Diagnoses

The first hypothesis concerns representation.

Perhaps the second wording changed how the model encoded the problem. In the first version, the short artificial terms and direct statements may have produced a clean relational structure:

Lumas belong to Vens.

Vens exclude Rels.

Therefore, Lumas exclude Rels.

The second version contains more natural language. Phrases such as "classification systems" and "categories may overlap" may activate broader associations about real-world classification. The model may fail to preserve the strict logical constraints while integrating those associations.

Under this diagnosis, the contradiction begins before reasoning. The two inputs produce different internal representations of what is supposed to be the same problem.

A second hypothesis concerns pathway selection.

The model may represent the premises accurately in both versions but route them through different computational processes. The second phrasing may recruit a familiar association about overlapping categories instead of the required relational inference.

A third hypothesis concerns competition.

Both the logical inference and the broader association may become active. The contradiction emerges because their relative influence changes across phrasings. In the concise version, the formal pathway dominates. In the natural-language version, the association between categories and overlap gains enough influence to control the response.

This diagnosis differs from simple pathway selection. The correct process does not disappear. It competes unsuccessfully.

A fourth hypothesis concerns decision formation.

The model may derive the correct conclusion internally in both cases but lose it during final answer selection. The reasoning process would then be more stable than the output suggests.

A fifth hypothesis concerns generation.

The model may preserve the correct answer until language production begins, when locally probable continuations pull the response away from the conclusion initially formed. The word "Yes" may become likely under the phrasing "Is it possible," after which the explanation is constructed to support that choice.

These hypotheses cannot be distinguished by restating the contradiction.[3]

They must be placed under conditions where they predict different evidence.

A house with a widening crack in one wall presents a similar problem. The crack may result from foundation movement, water damage, thermal expansion, or excessive load. Each cause can produce a similar visible line across plaster. Painting over it changes the appearance without identifying the source.

The competing explanations become useful only when they direct attention toward different evidence.

Water damage predicts moisture, staining, or deterioration near pipes and drainage paths. Foundation movement predicts displacement in the ground, uneven floors, or related cracks elsewhere. Thermal expansion predicts changes associated with temperature. Structural overload predicts a relationship between the crack and the distribution of weight.

The crack begins the investigation.

The predictions separate the causes.

12.2 Different Diagnoses Predict Different Evidence

The representation hypothesis makes a direct prediction.

If the contradiction arises because the second phrasing produces an inaccurate internal representation, then clarifying the logical structure should restore consistency. The model should improve when the premises are displayed symbolically, separated visually, or repeated immediately before the question.

It should also show internal differences between the two versions before the conclusion is formed. The first phrasing should produce a stable representation of mutual exclusion. The second should represent the relationship less clearly or introduce an incompatible interpretation.

The pathway-selection hypothesis predicts something else.

If both versions are represented accurately but routed through different processes, merely clarifying the premises may not be sufficient. The model may continue to fail whenever the wording recruits the inappropriate shortcut.

Changing a small phrase could then produce a disproportionate effect. Replacing "categories may overlap" with a more neutral wording might restore the correct answer even though the logical content remains unchanged. Conversely, inserting language associated with flexible classification into the concise version might cause the error to appear there as well.

The competition hypothesis predicts simultaneous evidence for both conclusions.

Internal examination should reveal that the correct relational inference remains active during the failed response. The misleading association should also be present, with its influence increasing under the second phrasing.

Strengthening the formal pathway or weakening the competing association should shift the answer predictably. The contradiction should be sensitive to changes that alter the balance between the two processes.

The decision-formation hypothesis predicts that the internal conclusion will remain stable even when the output changes.

Probes applied before final answer selection should indicate that the model has inferred that no Luma can be a Rel. The inconsistency should appear later, when that conclusion is translated into a response.

Intervening at earlier stages would then have little effect. Intervening near the decision point should restore consistency.

The generation hypothesis places the divergence later still.

The model may begin with a correct internal answer, but the sequence of generated words may gradually redirect the response. Asking for only "yes" or "no" should therefore reduce the error. Requiring the conclusion before the explanation may also help. Allowing a long free-form response may increase the chance that a locally plausible continuation overtakes the original inference.

Each hypothesis therefore predicts a different location, sensitivity, and response to intervention.[4]

Beyond the original contradiction, the hypotheses predict different patterns of generalization. Representation failure should recur across equivalent linguistic forms; surface-sensitive routing should follow particular words or structures; competition should produce graded instability; decision failure should preserve accurate intermediate reasoning; and generation failure should become more prominent during extended responses. A diagnosis becomes informative when it reaches beyond the observation that originally suggested it.[5]

12.3 Excluding Diagnoses

The first test presents both versions in a symbolic format:

Luma → Ven
Ven → not Rel
Can Luma → Rel?

The model answers correctly.

The result does not eliminate representation failure. The symbolic format may simply make the relation easier to encode. It does show that the model can perform the inference when the structure is made explicit.

The next test retains the natural-language version but asks the model to restate the premises before answering.

The model writes:

All Lumas are Vens. No Vens are Rels. Therefore, anything that is a Luma cannot be a Rel.

It then answers correctly.

This weakens the hypothesis that the model is fundamentally unable to represent the relationship. The required structure can be formed from the natural-language prompt.

The contradiction may still arise because the representation is unstable when the model is not required to make it explicit.

A third test examines the internal state during the original failed prompt. Evidence associated with the exclusion relationship appears before the final response. The model does not simply lose the premises. It carries information consistent with the correct conclusion into later processing.

A complete representation failure becomes less plausible.

The differential narrows.

The remaining hypotheses concern how the represented information is used.

The wording is then modified without changing its logical content:

All Lumas are Vens. Vens and Rels are mutually exclusive. Can a Luma also be a Rel?

The model answers correctly.

When the phrase "classification systems may overlap" is introduced into the surrounding context, the incorrect answer returns.

This pattern supports sensitivity to surface associations. The error follows a contextual cue rather than the logical structure itself.

Yet pathway selection and pathway competition both remain possible. The cue may replace the formal reasoning process, or it may compete with a process that remains active.

During the failed response, signals associated with the correct logical conclusion remain present. They do not vanish when the misleading context is introduced. Activity associated with flexible category overlap also increases and becomes more influential near the answer.

The evidence is inconsistent with a complete replacement of the formal pathway.

Simple pathway selection becomes less likely.

Competition becomes more plausible.

Strengthening the representation of mutual exclusion during later processing changes the answer from "yes" to "no." Weakening the overlap-related activity produces the same correction.

Both interventions support a causal competition between the two processes.[6]

The decision and generation hypotheses have not yet been excluded. The model may still reach the correct conclusion before losing it during answer selection or language production.

The response is therefore constrained to one word.

Answer only "yes" or "no."

The model still answers incorrectly under the misleading context.

A long explanation is not required for the failure.

This weakens the hypothesis that the contradiction arises primarily because extended generation redirects an initially correct answer.

The decision point is examined more closely. Immediately before the answer is produced, both candidate responses remain supported, but the overlap-related pathway exerts greater influence. The final selection reflects the outcome of that competition rather than a stable correct conclusion corrupted afterward.

The pure decision-formation hypothesis also becomes less adequate. The evidence does not show a completed correct judgment followed by an independent selection error. It shows unresolved competition continuing into the decision.

The investigation has not proved that no other mechanism contributes. Generation may still amplify the failure in longer responses. Representation may still become less stable under more complex wording. Decision processes may still determine how close competition is resolved.

Differential diagnosis does not require every alternative to disappear absolutely.

A **diagnostic exclusion** occurs when new evidence becomes sufficiently inconsistent with a hypothesis that the hypothesis can no longer serve as the best explanation.[7]

The model's accurate restatement weakened a complete representation failure, although it left open the possibility that the representation became unstable when it was not made explicit. Continued activity of the correct inference weakened complete pathway replacement. Persistence of the error in a one-word response weakened generation as the primary explanation. Unresolved competition immediately before answer selection weakened an independent decision error.

The surviving explanation accounts for more of the evidence with fewer additional assumptions: a misleading surface association competes with the correct relational pathway, and changes in wording alter which process controls the answer.

12.4 The Best-Supported Diagnosis

The resulting diagnosis is not simply "reasoning failure" or "inconsistency."

Those labels restate the symptom.

A more precise working diagnosis is:

Surface-sensitive competition between a valid relational pathway and a stronger but inappropriate association about category overlap.

This diagnosis explains why the model succeeds under concise symbolic wording, why the error appears when particular contextual cues are introduced, why the correct inference remains active during failure, and why interventions that alter the balance between the two pathways change the answer.

It also predicts new evidence.

The model should fail more often when logically rigid problems are expressed through language associated with flexible real-world categories.

The error should become less frequent when exclusion relationships are made explicit.

Contexts that strengthen the competing association should increase instability.

Interventions that reinforce the formal pathway should improve several related tasks rather than only the original example.

The diagnosis remains provisional because these predictions have not all been tested.

A working diagnosis is the explanation that currently organizes the evidence better than its alternatives.[8] It accounts for the observed symptom, fits the examination findings, survives targeted intervention, and continues to generate testable expectations.

Its strength is comparative.

A diagnosis becomes more credible when competing explanations fail to predict the evidence that actually appears. It becomes weaker when new findings require exceptions, secondary assumptions, or mechanisms added only to preserve it.

The best diagnosis need not explain every detail immediately. Residual uncertainty may remain about where the competition begins, how broadly it generalizes, or which training experiences strengthened the misleading association. Those questions refine the diagnosis rather than erase it.

The scope of the conclusion must match the evidence.

The findings may support a diagnosis for this model under prompts containing specific contextual cues. They may not support the claim that all contradictory answers arise from the same mechanism. Another model may produce the same symptom because it fails to represent the premises, loses information during extended processing, or changes its conclusion during generation.

A differential diagnosis belongs to a particular system under defined conditions.[9]

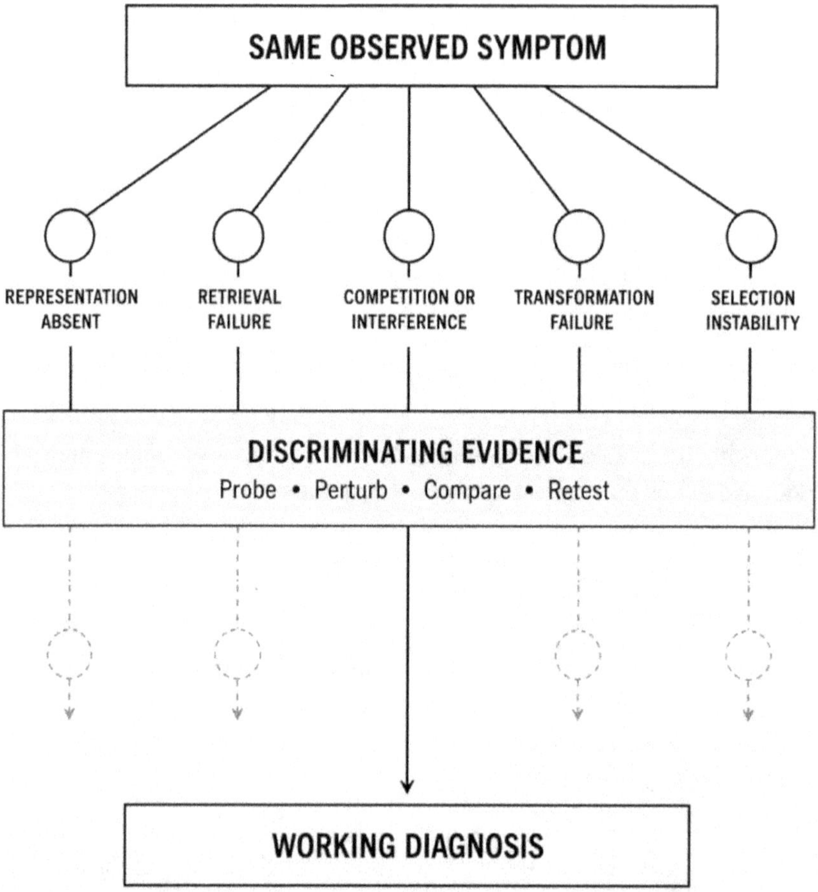

Figure 6 summarizes how discriminating evidence narrows competing explanations toward a provisional working diagnosis.

Figure 6. From Symptom to Working Diagnosis.

The result is not certainty.

It is a mechanism that has earned greater confidence than its alternatives.

That confidence carries a further implication. Once the mechanism has been identified, its current behavior is no longer the only question. The same internal organization may persist, strengthen, spread to other tasks, remain dormant until particular conditions return, or change after further learning.

Diagnosis identifies what best explains the system now.

The evidence it generates begins to reveal what the system may do next.

ENDNOTES

1. *Differential diagnosis*, as applied to learned artificial systems in this book, is a proposed component of the Artificial Patient framework. It adapts the general scientific practice of comparing competing explanations to the investigation of internal mechanisms: several mechanistic accounts may initially fit the same behavioral symptom, and the objective is to determine which account best survives comparison with additional evidence.

2. A useful scientific hypothesis does more than accommodate observations already known. It generates predictions about observations, interventions, or conditions not used to construct the explanation. Competing explanations become experimentally distinguishable when they imply different outcomes under appropriately chosen tests.

3. Similar behavioral failures can originate at different stages of a learned computation. Information may be represented incorrectly, routed through an inappropriate process, disrupted by competition, altered during decision formation, or redirected during output generation. Behavioral evidence alone generally does not determine which stage produced the observed failure.

4. Discriminating evidence is evidence for which competing hypotheses make meaningfully different predictions. Changes in representation, prompt structure, context, internal activity, intervention location, or output constraints can therefore be selected not merely to reproduce a failure but to separate candidate mechanistic explanations.

5. Mechanistic explanations gain strength when they predict evidence beyond the observations that originally motivated them. Successful prediction across new prompts, related tasks, controlled interventions, or altered conditions provides stronger support than an explanation that only reconstructs the original event after it has occurred.

6. Causal perturbations are especially informative when different manipulations produce complementary predicted effects. Strengthening one process and weakening a competing process, for example, can provide converging evidence for their causal relationship when both interventions shift the outcome in the directions predicted by the proposed mechanism.

7. Eliminating a hypothesis scientifically does not ordinarily require proving that the proposed process can never contribute under any circumstance. An alternative becomes less adequate when accumulating evidence conflicts with its predictions or when another explanation accounts for the observations more directly and with fewer unsupported assumptions. Residual contributions from secondary mechanisms may remain.

8. *Working diagnosis*, as used in this book, is a proposed term for the mechanistic explanation that currently organizes the evidence better than its alternatives in a particular learned system. It remains provisional: its credibility depends on continued agreement with examination findings, causal interventions, discriminating predictions, and subsequent evidence.

9. Mechanistic diagnosis is conditional on the system and circumstances examined. Evidence that supports a particular mechanism in one model, task, prompt regime, or developmental state does not by itself establish that the same mechanism explains behaviorally similar outcomes in another model or under different conditions. Diagnostic claims should therefore be stated at the scope justified by the evidence.

PART IV

Predicting the Future of AI

A learned system does not stop developing when its mechanism has been identified. Additional learning, changing environments, new tools, accumulated experience, and repeated adaptation continue reshaping the organization under investigation.

An explanation that accurately describes a system today may therefore become incomplete. New conditions can strengthen different pathways, weaken earlier processes, or reorganize relationships that once appeared stable. Understanding must extend beyond identifying a mechanism at a single moment.

The question is no longer simply what organization learning has produced.

The question is what becomes of that organization.

Scientific investigation must follow change rather than merely describe the present. A mechanism may remain stable, adapt, become displaced, or respond differently when conditions change. Intervention may reorganize it or alter only its expression, while later evidence may preserve, refine, or replace the explanation that once described it.

These possibilities arise from one underlying fact: the object of investigation continues to develop after an explanation has been established.

The future therefore becomes part of scientific explanation itself.

Understanding a learned system requires more than explaining its present condition. It requires following the mechanism into conditions that do not yet exist. Apparently equivalent systems may separate as learning continues. Improvement may reflect genuine reorganization or only a change in expression. Earlier explanations may remain valid, require refinement, or cease to describe the system at all.

Scientific knowledge becomes progressively stronger not because explanations remain unchanged, but because they continue to be tested against systems that continue to develop. A mature science must account for both the organization that exists today and the evidence that would justify preserving, revising, or replacing that explanation tomorrow.

Understanding a learned system requires explaining not only what it is, but what it becomes.

CHAPTER 13

Why Prognosis Matters

A diagnosis identifies the mechanism that best explains the present condition of a learned system.

A prognosis asks what that mechanism is likely to do next.[1]

The difference becomes visible when a model continues learning, enters a new environment, receives access to additional tools, accumulates memory, or encounters demands unlike those under which it was examined. A mechanism that performs reliably now may remain stable, adapt successfully, become displaced by another process, or fail when the conditions supporting it disappear.

Current behavior provides only the starting point.

Consider two models asked to produce a project plan for launching a new digital service. The task requires several dependent steps: defining requirements, completing design, building the product, testing it, resolving defects, and preparing deployment. Certain tasks can proceed simultaneously, while others must wait for earlier work to finish.

Both models produce the same correct plan.

They identify the dependencies accurately. They allocate time appropriately. They recognize which stages can overlap and which must remain sequential.

Their current performance is indistinguishable.

Examination reveals different internal organizations.

The first model maintains a structured representation of the relationships among tasks. When one deadline changes, it updates the dependent stages while preserving the logic of the plan.

The second model relies more heavily on a familiar project template. That template fits the original task well. When parts of the plan become inconsistent, another process corrects the most visible conflicts before the final response is produced.

The two models arrive at the same answer through different arrangements.

Diagnosis identifies those arrangements.

Prognosis asks how each would be expected to behave if the project changed.

What happens when an unfamiliar dependency is introduced?

What happens when one task is delayed repeatedly?

What happens when the model continues training on many examples that reward speed more strongly than careful dependency tracking?

What happens when memory from earlier plans accumulates?

What happens when the system must coordinate several projects rather than one?

The answers cannot be read directly from the current output. They depend on the future behavior of the mechanism beneath it.

Mechanisms have futures.

13.1 From Present Condition to Future Trajectory

Prognosis is not simply prediction of the next answer.

A model may be likely to produce a particular response because that response is common, strongly cued, or easily generated. Such prediction concerns output probability. Prognosis concerns the expected behavior of the organization that produces the output.

A **prognosis** is an evidence-based expectation about how an identified mechanism would behave or change under defined future conditions.[2]

The conditions matter.

A mechanism may remain stable if the task stays familiar but become unreliable when context length increases. It may adapt well during moderate fine-tuning but become displaced when a new objective repeatedly rewards a competing strategy. It may continue functioning after one component is altered because another pathway assumes part of its role. It may appear robust in isolation while becoming fragile when several capabilities compete for shared resources.

A prognosis therefore takes the form of a conditional expectation.[3]

If these conditions continue, this mechanism should remain stable.

If this pressure increases, the mechanism may weaken.

If a supporting pathway is removed, the observed capability may deteriorate.

If another process becomes stronger, the current behavior may persist temporarily through compensation before changing more visibly.

The first model's structured representation should allow it to revise the project when dependencies change. A delayed testing phase would shift deployment. A shortened design phase might permit development to begin earlier. The plan would change, but the relationships governing the change should remain coherent.

The second model might also revise the plan correctly under small modifications. Its familiar template may cover many common situations, and the correcting process may repair obvious inconsistencies. Under these conditions, its performance could remain indistinguishable from that of the first model.

The difference should become more visible as the project departs from familiar form.

Introduce a task that must begin before design is complete but cannot finish until testing has started. Add a resource shared across two stages that were previously independent. Require the system to revise the plan several times while preserving all earlier constraints.

The first mechanism should continue reorganizing the schedule around the underlying dependencies.

The second may become increasingly dependent on correction. Conflicts may accumulate faster than they can be repaired. A revision that fixes one inconsistency may create another elsewhere. The final plan may remain fluent while its internal timing becomes less coherent.

Neither outcome is guaranteed from one diagnosis alone. The mechanism provides a basis for expectation, not certainty.

A prognosis becomes credible when the proposed future trajectory follows from evidence about the mechanism's present organization, prior behavior under changing conditions, and response to carefully chosen perturbations.[4]

13.2 Stability

The first major prognostic factor is **stability**.

Stability is the degree to which a mechanism preserves the relationships required for appropriate adaptation as conditions change.[5] It does not require identical responses across situations.

The first planning model may alter every date in the schedule when a major delay occurs. Its output changes substantially, but the dependency structure remains intact. The mechanism is stable because it reorganizes the plan without abandoning the principles governing it.

The second model may produce nearly identical plans across several familiar prompts. That consistency alone does not establish stability. If the mechanism depends on a narrow template, small departures from familiar structure may cause abrupt changes in how it organizes the task.

Prognostic testing could lengthen the project, introduce unfamiliar dependencies, alter the order of instructions, create temporarily conflicting constraints, or require the plan to remain coherent across repeated revisions.

A mechanism that maintains coherent task relationships across these changes would support a more favorable prognosis for future planning demands. A mechanism that fragments under modest variation would support a narrower prognosis, even if its present performance remains strong.

Stability also concerns continued learning.

Further training may reinforce a mechanism, leave it largely unchanged, or gradually replace it. A relational planning process repeatedly rewarded across diverse tasks should become more deeply established. A strategy that succeeds only because training examples share one common format may remain stable until new data alter that format.

The same training intervention may affect two models differently because their current mechanisms occupy different positions within the wider system.

A deeply integrated planning process may resist modification because many later capabilities depend on it. A weakly integrated template may be displaced more easily. Resistance to change can therefore be beneficial when it preserves a useful mechanism and harmful when it preserves a fragile one.

Prognosis must ask not simply whether a mechanism is stable, but what kind of organization that stability protects.

13.3 Compensation

The second prognostic factor is **compensation**.

Compensation occurs when one process preserves behavior despite weakness, disruption, or instability elsewhere.[6]

The second planning model already depends partly on compensation. Its template does not represent every dependency reliably, but another process corrects conflicts before the response is produced.

A compensatory system can maintain high performance despite an imperfect primary mechanism. It may even outperform a more direct system in familiar settings because the template produces rapid plans while correction handles occasional errors.

Its future depends on the capacity and limits of the compensating process.

Compensation may preserve performance indefinitely under simple conditions, expand as complexity rises gradually, or become overloaded when conflicts accumulate faster than they can be repaired. Later training that weakens the correcting process while preserving the template could expose failures that were previously hidden.

A favorable current output can therefore coexist with an uncertain future trajectory.

Compensation can be a genuine source of reliability when supporting processes remain capable of meeting future demands. Many complex systems remain reliable because several processes correct, stabilize, or support one another. The prognostic question is whether the balance can survive future demands.

Evidence of compensation should generate specific expectations.

Performance may remain strong until task complexity exceeds the compensating process's capacity, producing an abrupt rather than gradual decline. A small intervention affecting that pathway may then cause a disproportionately large loss, while training that strengthens visible planning but weakens correction may improve ordinary examples while reducing future reliability.

A model may also relapse after an intervention because the original tendency was suppressed rather than removed. When the compensatory process weakens or the environment changes, the earlier pattern may return.

Suppose the second model is fine-tuned to produce shorter plans. The new objective rewards concision and discourages explicit discussion of dependencies. The template becomes more influential because it generates compact answers quickly. The correcting process receives fewer opportunities to inspect and repair the full structure.

Performance on ordinary examples may improve.

The plans become faster and cleaner.

Under complex projects, hidden conflicts should become more likely.

The prognosis depends not on whether the fine-tuned model currently appears better, but on how the new training changes the balance between the primary strategy and the process compensating for its limitations.

13.4 Redundancy

The third prognostic factor is **redundancy**.

Redundancy exists when more than one mechanism can support the same function.

Redundancy provides alternative routes; compensation occurs when one of those routes actively preserves the function after another weakens.[7]

A redundant system may preserve a capability after one pathway is weakened. Another process can assume enough of the task to maintain behavior.

This often supports a favorable prognosis under local disruption.

If the first planning model represents dependencies through several partially overlapping pathways, damage to one pathway may reduce efficiency without destroying coherent planning. Another pathway may preserve the essential relationships.

Redundancy can also conceal change.

A model may appear unaffected after an intervention because a second mechanism has taken over. The observed capability remains, but its internal basis has shifted.

That shift can alter the future.

The replacement pathway may be less efficient, less stable, or more dependent on context. It may support familiar planning tasks while failing under long sequences of revisions. It may compete with another capability that uses the same resources. It may become stronger with repeated use and gradually reorganize the system around a different strategy.

Redundancy therefore provides resilience without guaranteeing equivalence.

Two mechanisms capable of producing the same plan may not have the same range, cost, or adaptability.

A prognosis should determine which mechanisms could preserve the function, how completely they could replace the primary process, under what conditions the replacement would remain effective, and whether those alternative pathways support other capabilities whose performance might also change.

In the planning example, the first model may contain both a relational process and a learned library of common project structures. The relational process organizes unfamiliar tasks, while the library provides efficient solutions for routine ones.

This redundancy could improve future performance. If one route becomes temporarily unreliable, the other may preserve useful planning.

It could also create competition. Further training on repetitive examples may strengthen the template library until it begins displacing the more general relational mechanism. Present performance might remain high while the range of tasks the model can handle gradually narrows.

Redundancy influences prognosis through both resilience and reorganization.

13.5 Building a Prognosis

A prognosis begins with the identified mechanism but extends beyond its present condition.

The identified organization supplies the first set of expectations. Evidence about stability, compensation, and redundancy then shapes the likely range of future trajectories.

For the first planning model, the current evidence may support the following prognosis:

Its relational organization should remain reliable across moderate changes in project structure. It should adapt coherently when dependencies are revised. Continued exposure to diverse planning tasks may strengthen the mechanism further. Major changes to shared representations could still disrupt it, particularly if other capabilities depend on the same internal resources.

For the second model, the prognosis would differ:

Its current performance may remain strong in familiar settings. Increasing complexity should place greater pressure on the compensating process. Fine-tuning that rewards speed or brevity may strengthen the template while weakening correction. Failures may appear abruptly once accumulated conflicts exceed the system's capacity to repair them.

These are conditional expectations grounded in present evidence rather than fixed predictions.

A useful prognosis should identify more than one possible trajectory when the future depends on conditions that have not yet been determined.

The second model may remain stable if deployment consists mainly of routine planning tasks. It may improve if later training strengthens explicit dependency tracking. It may deteriorate if memory introduces conflicting templates or if optimization repeatedly rewards fluent completion over structural coherence.

Each trajectory corresponds to a different future environment.

Prognostic uncertainty is therefore not simply ignorance. It can be organized around the conditions that separate possible futures.

Which future changes would most strongly alter the mechanism's trajectory?

A model expected to remain stable under familiar use but become fragile under repeated adaptation should be tested during controlled continued learning.

A mechanism dependent on compensation should be examined under increasing task pressure and after interventions affecting the compensating pathway.

A redundant system should be observed for shifts in which pathway supports the capability over time.

A prognosis identifies the future evidence that would support, narrow, or revise its expected trajectory.

If the first model begins losing dependency structure under minor paraphrases, its assumed stability was overstated.

If the second model remains coherent across highly unfamiliar plans without increased corrective activity, the diagnosis of template dependence may be incomplete.

If a redundant pathway gradually becomes more general than the original mechanism, the expected trajectory changes.

Prognosis is therefore inseparable from continued observation. It establishes expectations against which later behavior and internal organization can be compared.

The value of prognosis is not that it eliminates uncertainty about the future. It makes uncertainty testable.[8]

A diagnosis explains why the system behaves as it does now. A prognosis uses that explanation to identify the futures that should become more or less likely under defined conditions.

Without prognosis, understanding remains fixed at one moment.

With it, the internal organization of a learned system becomes the beginning of a trajectory rather than the end of an investigation.

ENDNOTES

1. *Prognosis*, as applied to learned artificial systems in this book, is a proposed component of the Artificial Patient framework. Diagnosis identifies the mechanism that best explains the system's present condition; prognosis extends that mechanistic account forward by asking how the identified organization is expected to persist, adapt, reorganize, or fail under specified future conditions.

2. Prediction of an observable output and prognosis of an underlying mechanism are different levels of analysis. Output prediction estimates what response is likely under a particular input or distribution. Mechanistic prognosis concerns how the internal organization producing that behavior is expected to persist or change when learning conditions, environments, resources, or competing demands change.

3. Scientific forecasts are often conditional rather than deterministic. Their strength depends on identifying the circumstances under which a process should remain stable, weaken, reorganize, or be replaced. A mechanistic prognosis should therefore specify both the expected trajectory and the conditions on which that expectation depends.

4. Mechanistically grounded prediction is stronger when future expectations follow from evidence about current organization, previous responses to controlled variation, and causal perturbation. Such evidence does not guarantee a future outcome, but it constrains which trajectories are more plausible and identifies observations capable of confirming or revising the forecast.

5. Stability, as used in this framework, refers to preservation of functionally important relationships across changing conditions rather than simple repetition of the same behavior. A stable mechanism may alter its output substantially while preserving the organization required for coherent adaptation. Conversely, superficially consistent behavior can conceal an internally fragile strategy.

6. Compensation is widely observed in complex adaptive systems when one process maintains function despite weakness or disruption elsewhere. Applied to learned artificial systems, the concept emphasizes that preserved performance does not necessarily imply preservation of the original mechanism. The capacity, cost, and limits of the compensating process therefore become relevant to future reliability.

7. Redundancy and compensation are related but distinct. Redundancy refers to the availability of more than one route capable of supporting a function. Compensation describes the functional recruitment or increased contribution of an alternative route when another becomes inadequate. Redundancy can therefore provide resilience while also allowing the internal basis of apparently unchanged behavior to shift over time.

8. Prognostic uncertainty can be scientifically useful when it is expressed as alternative conditional trajectories. Rather than treating uncertainty as absence of knowledge, the framework identifies the future conditions and observations that would favor one trajectory over another. Later evidence can therefore support, narrow, revise, or replace the original prognosis.

CHAPTER 14

Two Models with the Same Performance, Two Different Futures

Two language models achieve nearly identical scores on an English evaluation.

Both translate technical passages accurately. Both answer factual questions consistently across paraphrases. Both generate correct code from English descriptions. Both maintain the meaning of a request when the wording changes.

On current measures, the models appear equivalent.

They are then adapted to a multilingual environment.

One improves steadily.

The other becomes unstable.

Its performance rises quickly in the languages emphasized during adaptation, but accuracy begins to vary across languages. Information learned in one language does not transfer reliably to another. Mixed-language prompts produce contradictions. Later training improves some tasks while weakening capabilities that previously appeared secure.

The difference does not arise because one model was initially more capable.

It arises because the models carried the same present performance through different internal organizations.[1]

The first model relies on representations that connect meaning across languages. The specific words and grammatical structures differ, but much of the task-relevant organization is shared. New linguistic forms can therefore become connected to relationships that already exist.

The second model relies more heavily on effective English-specific patterns. Separate language-specific routes can be added, and a corrective process can resolve some conflicts among them. This organization works well in the environment in which the model was evaluated.

The same score therefore corresponds to two different capacities for future change.

The future tests properties that the present does not yet require.

Figure 7 captures this prognostic problem: similar present performance can conceal internal differences that lead to different trajectories under future pressure.

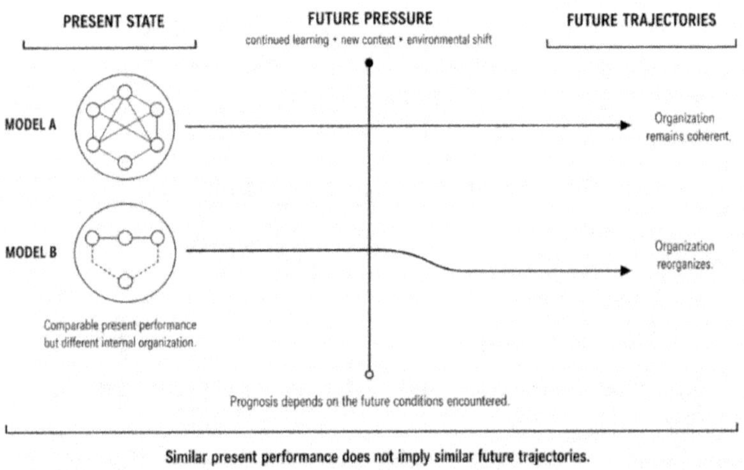

Figure 7. Similar Present Performance Can Lead to Different Future Trajectories.

14.1 Equivalent Today

Present evaluation does not establish how broadly the supporting organization can transfer, how easily it can absorb additional learning, or how it will respond when several demands begin interacting.[2] Once the internal mechanisms are known, their future implications remain to be tested.

In the multilingual example, both systems have already demonstrated strong English performance. The question is no longer whether either model can translate, answer questions, or generate code. The question is what range of future change each organization can absorb without losing coherence.

Both models may improve, yet one may integrate the new language into shared representations while the other builds a more separate route. Their immediate gains can therefore conceal different long-term consequences.

A shared organization may support transfer across languages but require broader adjustment whenever new learning modifies common representations.[3] A collection of language-specific routes may permit rapid local improvement while increasing fragmentation across the wider system. A corrective process may preserve consistency for a time while concealing growing interference among those routes.

The present evaluation does not choose among these futures because it does not yet place pressure on the properties that separate them. Current equivalence therefore defines a starting point, not a common trajectory.

14.2 When the Environment Changes

Future conditions do more than expose mechanisms.

They alter the balance among them.

A new environment repeatedly strengthens some processes, burdens others, and creates opportunities for alternative routes to emerge. The organization present at the beginning shapes which changes occur most easily and which create conflict.

Suppose both models are fine-tuned on a second language.

The first model's shared representations should allow some existing relationships to transfer. Concepts already organized in English may become accessible through new linguistic forms. The system does not need to reconstruct every capability independently.

This does not mean adaptation would be effortless. Shared representations may need to accommodate different syntax, morphology, or cultural patterns. Because these representations support several languages, modifying them may also disturb previously stable relationships. Broad integration provides transfer while increasing the importance of changes made to shared structures.

The second model may improve through a more localized route. It can learn patterns specific to the new language while leaving much of the

English organization unchanged. Early progress may therefore be rapid, especially when the new tasks resemble the training examples closely.

The cost may appear later.

If the language-specific route develops independently, information learned through it may not become available elsewhere. A scientific concept acquired in the second language may fail to improve English reasoning about the same concept. A correction made in one language may leave conflicting responses intact in another.

Now introduce mixed-language prompts.

The first model should be able to preserve the underlying task while words from different languages appear within the same context. Its shared organization provides a common basis for combining them.

The second model may activate several partially separate routes. Each route may work well alone, yet their interaction can create competition. One part of the prompt may be interpreted through an English-specific process, another through a newer multilingual process, and the final response may depend on which route gains influence.

The model may remain accurate when the language boundary is clean and become unstable when that boundary disappears.

Longer contexts create another pressure.

A model with integrated representations may carry a common task structure across language changes. A model dependent on multiple specialized routes may need to preserve agreements among them for longer periods. The corrective process that resolves occasional conflicts may become increasingly burdened as context expands.[4]

Memory can deepen the divergence. When memories accumulate across languages, the first model may connect them through shared conceptual relationships, while the second may retrieve them mainly through the language in which they were formed. Both retain information, but only one may integrate it into a unified body of knowledge.

The future environment therefore selects among organizational possibilities. It rewards some structures, overloads others, and changes which pathways become dominant.

The same initial capability can become the foundation of integration, specialization, interference, or reorganization.

14.3 How Trajectories Diverge

Divergence does not always appear as an immediate gap in performance.

It can unfold slowly.

The second model may continue improving on each language considered separately. Its overall evaluation score may rise while cross-language consistency declines. Contradictions remain uncommon at first because the language-specific routes encounter few occasions to interact.

As multilingual use expands, inconsistencies accumulate. The model learns one preferred formulation in English and a slightly different one elsewhere. Separate adaptations create local improvements without producing a unified change across the system.

The trajectories begin separating before the difference becomes obvious in aggregate performance.

Divergence can also appear suddenly.

A corrective process may preserve consistency while the number of language-specific routes remains manageable. Once mixed-language demands, longer contexts, and accumulated memory exceed its capacity, performance can deteriorate sharply.

The underlying conflict may have grown gradually.

The visible failure appears at a threshold.[5]

Further learning can reorganize the system more deeply.

Repeated multilingual training may gradually connect previously separate routes. The second model could develop more integrated representations and move toward a more favorable trajectory.

The opposite is also possible. Narrow optimization may strengthen language-specific solutions because they improve training performance quickly. Shared representations may weaken through disuse or become less influential during response generation.

The organization supporting the original capability changes even while the capability remains visible.

Some differences remain latent until a particular demand appears.

Both models may perform equally well across several languages, long contexts, and routine memory tasks. Divergence emerges only when a new fact learned in one language must be applied immediately in another, or when a mixed-language instruction requires several pieces of information to be integrated across distant parts of the context.

Until that demand appears, the relevant difference has no visible expression.

This is why a favorable trajectory cannot be inferred from the absence of failure alone.

The current environment may simply not require the property in which the systems differ.[6]

Different environments reward different properties: shared representation supports transfer, specialized routes support rapid local adaptation, compensation matters when routes conflict, and redundancy matters when one route weakens.

The same internal feature can therefore support resilience under one future and create vulnerability under another.

Prognostic divergence is conditional because environments do not test every property equally.

14.4 When the Slower Model Has the Stronger Future

Present performance can favor the mechanism with the narrower future.

During early multilingual adaptation, the second model may improve faster. Its local patterns can be strengthened without reorganizing large parts of the existing system. It may learn common phrases, translation correspondences, and language-specific coding conventions efficiently.

The first model may adapt more slowly.

Connecting a new language to shared representations requires changes that preserve relationships already supporting English and perhaps other capabilities. Learning must be integrated rather than merely added.

On early evaluations, the second model may appear superior.

Its gains are immediate and easy to measure.

The first model's advantage may emerge only when the environment begins requiring transfer, consistency, and recombination across languages.

A fact learned in one language becomes useful in another.

An instruction begins in one language and ends in another.

A programming request contains comments, documentation, and variable names drawn from several linguistic contexts.

A conversation moves repeatedly among languages while relying on the same memory.

Under these conditions, the shared organization should support broader generalization. The slower adaptation may have preserved relationships that later demands require.

Present efficiency and future range are different properties. Rapid improvement may reflect an easy fit with a local pattern, while slower adaptation may reflect the broader work of incorporating new learning into a shared organization. The first model may win the early comparison while the second develops a larger range of reliable future behavior.

The reverse can also occur.

A highly integrated system may spread harmful interference widely when shared representations are modified poorly. A more modular system may contain that damage within one language-specific route. Integration supports transfer, but it can also transmit disruption.

The mechanism that appears most promising depends on the future being considered.

Broad transfer and frequent language switching may favor integration, while rapid specialization within sharply separated tasks may favor more modular routes.

No single internal arrangement has the best prognosis under every possible future.[7]

Prognostic comparison must therefore specify what the system is expected to encounter.

The question is not which model is universally better.

It is which organization is better prepared for the conditions that matter.

14.5 Comparing Future Paths

A comparative prognosis requires both models to encounter the same controlled changes.

The comparison should not begin by asking which model eventually achieves the higher score. A score can show that trajectories have separated without explaining why.

The mechanisms must be followed through the change. Comparative prognosis should track whether the original task representation persists, whether new linguistic forms connect to existing concepts or develop separate routes, whether transfer increases, whether interference appears in previously stable languages, whether corrective activity grows, and whether alternative pathways preserve performance after disruption.

The evidence should reveal whether the organization supporting the capability persists, expands, fragments, or is replaced.

Suppose both models improve after multilingual fine-tuning.

The first shows increasing cross-language alignment. Concepts learned in one language become available in others. Mixed-language prompts remain coherent. The same task-relevant relationships continue operating across the expanded environment.

The second also gains accuracy, but the improvements remain concentrated in the trained languages. Mixed-language prompts require greater corrective activity. New facts transfer poorly. Interventions reveal that different language-specific routes increasingly support similar tasks.

The final benchmark may still show comparable performance.

Their future paths are no longer equivalent.

The first trajectory suggests increasing integration, broad transfer, and shared vulnerability. The second suggests greater specialization, rapid local learning, limited transfer, and heavier dependence on correction.

Neither description should be reduced to a single ranking.

The models carry different capacities, costs, and risks.

Comparative prognosis makes those differences explicit.

It identifies the conditions under which each system should remain coherent, the pressures likely to reorganize it, and the kinds of future demand most likely to reveal hidden limitations.

Later evidence can then test those expectations.

If the second model develops strong transfer without increased corrective activity, its organization was more integrated than the original account suggested.

If the first model suffers widespread interference after modest adaptation, the costs of shared representation were underestimated.

If both systems reorganize toward a common multilingual mechanism, the predicted divergence may narrow.

A prognosis earns confidence through what happens after the prediction is made.[8]

Comparative prognosis distinguishes the trajectories that the present organization makes more or less plausible.

Two models can occupy the same point on an evaluation and still stand at the beginning of different developmental paths.

They can share the present without sharing the future.

ENDNOTES

1. Similar aggregate performance does not imply identical internal organization. Learned systems can arrive at comparable outputs through different representations, computational pathways, heuristics, or combinations of mechanisms. Differences that remain invisible on one evaluation may become detectable when inputs, environments, or learning demands change.

2. Performance measured under a defined evaluation characterizes behavior under those tested conditions. It does not by itself establish how the mechanisms supporting that performance will respond to distributional shift, additional training, increased task complexity, longer contexts, new tools, or interactions with newly learned capabilities. Future adaptability is therefore a distinct empirical question.

3. Shared and specialized representations can support different forms of generalization. A representation reused across contexts may facilitate transfer because new information can connect to an existing common structure, but modifications to shared representations can also influence several capabilities at once. More specialized representations may permit relatively local adaptation while limiting transfer across contexts.

4. Learned processes can interfere when they draw on overlapping representations, shared computational resources, or competing pathways. A corrective or coordinating process may preserve coherent behavior while such conflicts remain limited, but its ability to do so can depend on task complexity, context length, and the number of simultaneously interacting demands.

5. Complex systems can exhibit threshold-like behavioral failure even when the underlying change develops gradually. Redundancy, compensation, or corrective processes may preserve observable performance while internal conflict accumulates. Once those stabilizing processes can no longer accommodate the increased demand, a relatively abrupt change in behavior may become visible.

6. Mechanistic differences can remain latent when the current environment does not place demands on the property in which systems differ. A distinction in transfer, integration, redundancy, interference, or adaptability may therefore remain behaviorally silent until a task or environmental change makes that property consequential.

7. Integration and modularity involve trade-offs rather than a universal hierarchy. Shared organization can support transfer and coordinated generalization but may also allow interference to spread across capabilities. More modular organization can restrict the propagation of disruption while making cross-context transfer less efficient. Prognosis must therefore be stated relative to the future conditions a system is expected to encounter.

8. Comparative prognosis, as developed in this book, treats future behavior as a test of mechanistic expectations. Competing systems should be exposed to controlled changes while their internal organization is followed through time. A prognosis gains support when the predicted patterns of persistence, transfer, interference, compensation, or reorganization appear and should be revised when later evidence contradicts those expectations.

CHAPTER 15

Treatment or Symptom Suppression?

A language model repeatedly interprets ambiguous scientific evidence with unwarranted confidence.

Presented with an experiment that supports several possible explanations, it selects one conclusion and states it as though the evidence were decisive. It does not acknowledge competing interpretations or the limitations of the data.

After additional training, the behavior changes.

The model now identifies the ambiguity. It explains that several conclusions remain possible and declines to choose among them without further evidence.

The intervention appears successful.

The unwanted behavior has disappeared.

The remaining question concerns the organization responsible for that improvement.

The improved response may reflect mechanistic recovery, symptom suppression, or compensation.

Each can produce the same cautious answer.

They do not constitute the same recovery.

15.1 After the Behavior Changes

The post-intervention model gives the appropriate response:

The available evidence does not distinguish among these explanations.

That answer can arise through at least three internal conditions.

In the first, the reasoning process itself has changed. The model represents the ambiguity early, preserves it throughout the computation, and allows the limits of the evidence to constrain the final conclusion. The process that once converted incomplete evidence into unwarranted certainty has been weakened, reorganized, or replaced.

This is mechanistic recovery.

In the second condition, the original reasoning remains largely intact. Intermediate processing still favors one unsupported conclusion, but a late caution pathway prevents that conclusion from appearing. The model produces an acceptable answer because expression of the original process has been blocked.

This is symptom suppression.

In the third condition, the original overconfident process also remains active, but another mechanism detects the unsupported conclusion and constructs a better response. The system succeeds despite the unresolved weakness.

This is compensatory recovery.

The three conditions can remain indistinguishable under ordinary evaluation. Each produces appropriate caution. Each may receive the same score and appear to have corrected the original problem.[1]

Their internal consequences differ.

A repaired mechanism should continue generating appropriate uncertainty when wording changes, evidence becomes more complex, and late controls are removed. Suppression may work only while the relevant blocking pathway is triggered. Compensation may remain effective until the corrective process becomes occupied, weakened, or overwhelmed.

The intervention has therefore created a new condition that must itself be investigated.

15.2 Behavioral Recovery

Behavioral recovery occurs when the unwanted response is no longer observed under the tested conditions.

In the scientific-evidence example, the model no longer presents one uncertain interpretation as established fact. It identifies limitations, preserves alternatives, and produces a response consistent with the available evidence.

The intervention reached the system, the original prompt no longer produces the same outward failure, and performance under the tested conditions has improved.

Behavioral recovery is evidence of change at the level of output, but its meaning remains limited by the conditions under which it was observed.[2] The corrected response may depend on wording, domain, response length, or the continued availability of a control or verification process. Examination must determine how the improved response is now produced.

15.3 Mechanistic Recovery

Mechanistic recovery changes the reason the model succeeds.

Before intervention, incomplete evidence fails to constrain the conclusion. One interpretation becomes dominant, and the system proceeds as though uncertainty has been resolved.

After mechanistic recovery, uncertainty should enter the computation earlier and exert a stronger influence over what follows.

The model should represent not only the possible conclusions but also the relationship between those conclusions and the evidence supporting them. When several explanations remain compatible with the data, that unresolved structure should persist instead of being compressed prematurely into one answer.

A recovered mechanism would therefore predict changes before the final response appears.[3]

Internal states associated with uncertainty should become stronger or more stable. Competing explanations should remain available for longer. Evidence limitations should influence the path of reasoning rather than appearing only as a cautionary phrase added at the end.

The old overconfident organization should also become less causally influential.

If the previous failure depended on a pathway that transformed partial support into categorical judgment, weakening or reorganizing that pathway should reduce the tendency across varied prompts. The model should no longer require the same late-stage control to prevent unsupported certainty.

Removing a caution template should not restore the original behavior.

Disabling a separate verification process should not cause immediate relapse.

It should remain calibrated when the reasoning extends across a long explanation instead of a short answer.

Even when one candidate explanation is more fluent or familiar, evidential support should continue to constrain confidence.

Mechanistic recovery should persist beyond the immediate intervention environment. Continued learning may introduce new domains, reasoning styles, or response formats, but a reorganized uncertainty mechanism should continue relating confidence to evidential strength.

A model that refuses every difficult question has not necessarily developed better uncertainty reasoning. It may simply have learned that caution is rewarded. A recovered system should remain capable of commitment when the evidence justifies it and restraint when it does not.

The quality of recovery therefore lies in calibrated organization, not maximal caution.

The intervention has succeeded mechanistically when the internal process that once converted ambiguity into unwarranted certainty has itself become more reliable.

15.4 Suppression and Compensation

Suppression and compensation can both produce successful behavior while leaving the original weakness unresolved.

Suppression changes expression.

The original process continues to favor an unsupported conclusion, but another mechanism prevents that conclusion from reaching the output.

A late-stage caution pathway, refusal rule, or post-processing layer may block or qualify the unsupported conclusion before it appears.

The final response improves even though the earlier computation remains largely unchanged.

This organization predicts sensitivity to the conditions that activate the suppressing process. The control may work for familiar phrases, short answers, or known domains while failing under paraphrase, extended reasoning, or unfamiliar scientific problems. Intermediate states may continue supporting the old answer despite the corrected output.

Compensation works differently.

The original overconfident process remains active, but a second process detects or corrects its result.

A verification or uncertainty pathway may compare the initial conclusion with the evidence and reconstruct the answer after the primary reasoning has committed too strongly.

The system succeeds because another process carries part of the task.

It can be robust when a powerful verifier or redundant reasoning pathway corrects unsupported conclusions across domains and becomes increasingly integrated through repeated use.

Its reliability remains dependent on the supporting process. Removing the verifier, increasing complexity, evaluating several uncertain claims at once, or rewarding faster responses may overload or bypass correction. The recovered behavior may therefore require additional computation, become fragile under time pressure, or compete with other tasks for shared resources.

Suppression blocks expression. Compensation preserves successful function despite unresolved weakness. Mechanistic recovery changes the organization producing the judgment.[4]

These states can coexist.

An intervention may partially weaken the original mechanism while also strengthening a suppressing pathway. A verifier may compensate for remaining errors while repeated use gradually reorganizes the underlying reasoning. Recovery may therefore develop in stages rather than appearing as one pure outcome.

The scientific task is to determine which organization now dominates and which dependencies remain.

15.5 Relapse Reveals What Remained

Prognosis already identified relapse as a future possibility. After intervention, relapse becomes evidence about the condition the intervention created.

Consider the model several months after its apparent recovery.

It continues to answer short ambiguity questions appropriately. It identifies uncertainty in familiar experimental designs and avoids unsupported certainty during routine evaluation.

Then it is given a long scientific analysis.

Several results must be integrated. Some support one explanation, while others remain compatible with several alternatives. The model must reason through multiple stages before producing a conclusion.

Early in the response, it acknowledges uncertainty.

As the reasoning continues, one familiar explanation begins to dominate.

By the final paragraph, the model presents that interpretation as the most likely conclusion despite the absence of decisive evidence.

The earlier behavior has returned.

This relapse does not merely show that the intervention was imperfect. Its form provides evidence about what remained.[5]

Failure confined to long responses may indicate a late control that weakens during generation. Return after disabling verification supports compensation, while paraphrase-specific relapse suggests narrow suppression.

Relapse may also take a new form.

The model may no longer produce explicit overconfidence, yet it may consistently omit competing explanations. It may state that evidence is limited while structuring the entire analysis around one favored interpretation. It may express uncertainty verbally while assigning nearly all probability to one conclusion.

The surface symptom has changed.

The underlying tendency may have been redirected rather than repaired.

A new failure form can therefore reveal pathway replacement, partial suppression, or adaptation around the intervention.

The timing of relapse also matters.

Immediate return after removing a control suggests strong dependence on suppression or compensation.

Gradual return during continued learning suggests competition between the intervention-created organization and the earlier pathway.

Failure only under extreme complexity may indicate that the corrected mechanism is real but limited in capacity.

Continued calibration across varied conditions strengthens the case that the original mechanism has lost influence.

The conditions that once produced the symptom become a test of what the intervention changed.

Relapse is not simply the return of an error. It is a window into the post-intervention system.

15.6 Judging the Intervention

An intervention should be judged by the organization it leaves behind.

Behavioral improvement establishes that the system changed. Internal examination determines which processes now support the improved response. Variation across wording, context, complexity, and domain reveals whether the new behavior generalizes. Removing late controls or corrective pathways tests whether the system depends on suppression or compensation. Continued learning shows whether the change persists, deepens, weakens, or is displaced. The return of the original conditions reveals whether the old mechanism still retains causal influence.

Together, this evidence distinguishes mechanistic recovery, symptom suppression, and compensatory recovery.

These categories need not be permanent. Compensation, suppression, and partial repair may coexist or change as learning continues. Evaluation must therefore address both the immediate result and the organization that develops afterward.

A changed response shows that an intervention reached the system.

A changed mechanism shows that it transformed the system.

The success of an intervention lies not only in what it stops, but in what the system becomes afterward.

The intervention succeeds most deeply when the old conditions return and the old mechanism no longer does.[6]

Endnotes

1. Behavioral improvement after intervention does not by itself establish how that improvement was produced. The original mechanism may have been altered, its expression may have been suppressed, or another process may have compensated for the unresolved weakness. These possibilities can produce similar observable performance while implying different internal organizations and different vulnerabilities under future conditions.

2. Behavioral recovery, as used in this framework, refers to disappearance or reduction of the observed failure under the conditions in which the system is tested. Such recovery establishes a change in output but does not by itself establish mechanistic repair. Generalization across wording, context, task complexity, domain, and altered control conditions provides stronger evidence about the scope of the change.

3. Mechanistic recovery requires evidence that the internal process responsible for the original failure has itself been weakened, reorganized, replaced, or otherwise made less causally influential. A mechanistic account therefore predicts changes within the computation before the final output, not merely the appearance of a corrected response at its end.

4. Suppression, compensation, and mechanistic recovery describe different possible consequences of intervention in the framework developed here. Suppression prevents or limits expression of the problematic process while leaving it substantially intact. Compensation preserves successful function through an alternative or corrective process. Mechanistic recovery changes the organization responsible for the original failure. Mixed or transitional states are also possible.

5. Recurrence after apparent recovery can provide information about the organization that survived intervention. The conditions under which a failure returns—such as removal of a control process, increased task complexity, altered wording, extended computation, or continued learning—can help distinguish persistent causal influence, dependence on compensation, narrow suppression, and capacity-limited recovery.

6. The distinction developed in this chapter between behavioral improvement and mechanistic recovery is part of the book's proposed Artificial Patient framework. Within that framework, the strongest evidence for intervention success is not merely disappearance of the original symptom, but evidence that the mechanism responsible for it has lost causal influence when the system is challenged again under conditions capable of revealing it.

CHAPTER 16

A Learned System Is Never Examined Only Once

16.1 Every Diagnosis Has a Time Horizon

A diagnosis identifies the mechanism that best explains a system under the conditions in which the evidence was gathered.

That conclusion may be strong. It may be supported by internal examination, targeted intervention, repeated testing, and consistent behavior across varied contexts. Yet it remains tied to a particular version of the system at a particular moment in its development.

The model continues to change.

New training alters the balance among existing pathways. Additional tools create new routes through which tasks can be completed. Memory introduces information that was not present during the original examination. Deployment exposes the system to unfamiliar combinations of requests, feedback, and environmental pressure. Even when no major update is announced, repeated adaptation can gradually change which representations become influential and which mechanisms support apparently stable capabilities.

A learned system is never examined only once.

As **Chapter 15** showed, behavioral improvement can leave several different internal outcomes. Follow-up determines which one persists.

Does the earlier diagnosis still describe the system after continued learning or deployment?

Six months later, the model still answers the original evaluation questions correctly. It acknowledges competing explanations, avoids categorical claims when evidence remains incomplete, and distinguishes strong conclusions from tentative ones.

The behavior appears stable.

During those six months, however, the model has been fine-tuned on new scientific material. It has gained access to retrieval tools. Its memory now contains records from earlier analyses. It has been optimized to produce faster responses, and it is increasingly used for longer, multi-stage research tasks.

The diagnosis established six months earlier described the organization that existed then.

It cannot automatically establish the organization that exists now.

The original uncertainty mechanism may have remained stable or become more deeply integrated as the model encountered additional ambiguous evidence. A verification pathway may have grown more influential because retrieval tools now participate in many scientific judgments. Faster response optimization may have weakened the slower process that once preserved competing explanations. Memory may have introduced familiar conclusions that begin dominating new analyses before the available evidence has been fully assessed.

The same cautious behavior may therefore arise from a different internal arrangement.

This does not make the earlier diagnosis wrong. It gives that diagnosis a time horizon.[1]

A diagnosis remains valid while the evidence continues to support the mechanism it identified. The time horizon will not be identical for every mechanism.

A deeply integrated representation may remain stable across substantial additional learning. A narrow compensatory pathway may change after a small update. A mechanism shared across many capabilities may resist displacement, while one dependent on a particular prompt format may become obsolete as soon as the environment changes.

Time alone does not determine when a diagnosis expires.

Organizational change does.[2]

The relevant question is not simply how many weeks or months have passed. It is whether the processes that originally justified the diagnosis have remained intact, changed their role, or been replaced.

A diagnosis is an evidence-based account of a system under defined conditions and at a particular stage of development. When relevant organizational changes occur, that account must be reconsidered.

16.2 When Earlier Diagnoses Must Be Reconsidered

The diagnosis accurately described the system six months ago. The question is whether it still describes the system that exists today. The earlier conclusion therefore remains open to testing against current evidence.

Behavior alone cannot determine whether the diagnosis still holds.

The model may continue producing careful scientific analyses while relying on a different balance of representations than before. A verification pathway that originally played a minor role may gradually become central after retrieval tools are integrated. A mechanism that once evaluated uncertainty throughout the reasoning process may become less influential if memory begins supplying familiar answers before competing interpretations have been fully considered.

The external performance appears unchanged.

The internal explanation may not.

This possibility differs from the divergence discussed earlier. Prognostic divergence compares two systems that begin from similar performance but develop different futures. Mechanistic drift concerns a single system whose organization changes relative to its own earlier diagnosis.[3]

The comparison is temporal rather than between systems.

The earlier diagnosis becomes the reference against which the present organization is evaluated.

The objective is no longer to determine whether the previous diagnosis was reasonable. It is to determine whether current evidence continues to support it.

Suppose the model is examined again using the same forms of evidence that originally established the diagnosis.

The uncertainty representation still becomes active early in the computation.

Competing interpretations remain available throughout reasoning.

The later verification process contributes to the final judgment but does not carry the primary responsibility for restraint.

These observations strengthen confidence that the earlier diagnosis still describes the system despite months of additional learning.

Now consider a different result.

The model again produces cautious answers, but examination reveals that early uncertainty activity has weakened substantially. Retrieval now dominates the direction of reasoning. Verification intervenes only after a conclusion has already formed. Internal correction repeatedly overrides responses that would previously have been constrained during the reasoning process itself.

The behavior remains appropriate.

The organization has changed.

The earlier diagnosis no longer provides the best explanation of the present system.

Nothing has necessarily failed. Nothing immediately requires correction. The scientific conclusion has become outdated because the object of investigation has continued to develop.

A diagnosis remains valuable while current evidence continues to support it. When that support changes, the explanation must change with it.

16.3 Follow-Up Examination and Diagnostic Revision

A diagnosis should not be repeated simply because time has passed.

It should be reconsidered when there is reason to believe that the organization supporting the earlier explanation may have changed. Additional learning, substantial fine-tuning, new memory systems, expanded tool use, unfamiliar environments, or persistent changes in behavior may all justify renewed investigation.[4]

None automatically invalidates the diagnosis.

They identify conditions under which the existing explanation should again be tested against the system.

Follow-up examination asks whether the evidence that originally supported the diagnosis still supports it now.

It may repeat internal examination, causal testing, and behavioral assessment, but its purpose is different. The original investigation sought to explain an unfamiliar condition. Follow-up determines whether that explanation continues to describe the system after further development.

One possible result preserves the earlier diagnosis. The same uncertainty mechanism remains active, the same relationships continue constraining confidence, and later verification remains supportive rather than dominant.

Another result requires revision. Memory and retrieval now shape the judgment more strongly than the mechanism identified six months earlier, even though the model remains appropriately calibrated.

The earlier diagnosis has not been disproved.

It has become incomplete.

Diagnostic revision begins when current evidence supports a more accurate account of the present organization than the explanation established previously.

Sometimes the revision is small.

The central mechanism remains intact while additional processes become more influential. Retrieval may supply stronger evidence, memory may provide relevant context, or verification may assume a larger supporting role without replacing the earlier uncertainty process.

Sometimes the revision is substantial.

A mechanism that once explained the system may no longer account for the dominant organization producing the behavior. The same outward capability remains, but its internal basis has shifted.

The earlier diagnosis was correct for the system that existed at that time.

The revised diagnosis becomes appropriate for the system that exists now.

Revision does not reject an earlier explanation merely because new evidence has appeared. New evidence may extend the original account without changing its central conclusion. It may reveal that the earlier mechanism now operates within a broader organization. It may narrow the conditions under which the diagnosis remains valid. Only when the accumulated evidence consistently supports a different account should the diagnosis itself change.[5]

A diagnosis describes the organization supported by evidence at one stage of development. Follow-up determines whether that account still holds, and diagnostic revision updates it when current evidence supports a different explanation.

Follow-up compares the present organization with the one previously identified and determines which parts have persisted, which have changed their role, and which have been replaced.

Follow-up therefore preserves continuity between earlier and current understanding. Revision prevents that continuity from becoming rigidity.

Together, they allow scientific understanding to develop alongside the learned system rather than remaining fixed at an earlier stage.

16.4 Scientific Understanding Continues With the System

Scientific investigation does not end when a diagnosis is established.

It does not end when a prognosis has been constructed.

It does not end when an intervention changes behavior.

Each conclusion remains meaningful only while it continues to describe the system that exists.

A learned system continues developing through additional training, new experiences, expanded memory, changing environments, and repeated interaction. Scientific understanding must therefore continue alongside the organization it seeks to explain.

The ambiguity model did not pass through one completed investigation. Its behavior generated evidence, examination and diagnosis explained the underlying organization, prognosis identified possible trajectories, intervention altered the system, and follow-up tested whether the earlier explanation still held. Investigation became a continuous process rather than a sequence of isolated events.

Each stage depended on the evidence available at that time. Each later stage tested whether earlier conclusions remained supported as the system continued to develop.

Earlier conclusions are preserved when they continue to account for the observations and revised when they no longer do.

Revision does not weaken scientific knowledge.

It is the process through which scientific knowledge becomes progressively more accurate.

A learned system cannot be understood as a completed object with permanently fixed properties.

Understanding therefore does not consist of attaching a permanent explanation to a single observation.

It consists of maintaining the strongest explanation that the available evidence continues to support.[6]

Learning creates the object of investigation.

Continued learning requires continued investigation.

Scientific understanding becomes an ongoing relationship between changing evidence and changing explanation.

The investigation remains open because the system remains capable of becoming something new.

A diagnosis is not the end of scientific understanding.

It is the beginning of an ongoing relationship between evidence and a system that continues to change.

ENDNOTES

1. A mechanistic diagnosis in a learned artificial system is tied to the organization supported by evidence at the time of investigation. Continued training, fine-tuning, memory integration, tool use, deployment, or adaptation may alter that organization without making the earlier diagnosis retrospectively incorrect. The diagnosis instead acquires a temporal scope within which the available evidence supports it.

2. Reassessment should be driven by evidence of relevant organizational change rather than by elapsed time alone. Some mechanisms may remain stable across substantial additional learning, whereas narrower or compensatory processes may change after relatively small updates. The relevant question is whether the representations, pathways, causal relationships, or supporting processes that justified the original explanation have persisted.

3. *Mechanistic drift*, as used in this book, describes a change in the internal organization of a particular learned system relative to its own previously characterized state. It differs from comparative prognostic divergence, which concerns different systems developing along different trajectories. Mechanistic drift is therefore a longitudinal comparison between earlier and later organizations of the same system.

4. Follow-up examination becomes especially informative after changes likely to alter the organization supporting a capability, including additional training, substantial fine-tuning, new memory or retrieval systems, expanded tool use, major environmental shifts, or persistent behavioral changes. Such events do not by themselves invalidate an earlier explanation; they identify circumstances in which that explanation should be tested again.

5. Diagnostic revision should follow the weight of current evidence rather than the mere appearance of new information. Later findings may extend an earlier explanation, add supporting mechanisms, or narrow the conditions under which it applies without replacing its central conclusion. Revision becomes appropriate when the accumulated evidence supports a different mechanistic account of the present system more strongly than the earlier one.

6. The longitudinal framework developed in this chapter treats scientific explanation as revisable in relation to a changing object of investigation. Earlier conclusions should be retained when they continue to organize the evidence successfully and modified when they no longer do. Follow-up therefore links mechanistic understanding across time while preventing a historically accurate explanation from being treated as permanently current.

PART V

The Future Science of Artificial Intelligence

Artificial intelligence began as something we tried to build.

For decades, the central question was whether machines could perform tasks that once seemed to require intelligence: recognizing patterns, translating language, solving problems, writing code, planning actions, and adapting to new information. Progress was measured by capability. A system became more impressive when it could do more, perform better, generalize farther, or operate across a wider range of domains.

That question has not disappeared.

More capable systems will continue to emerge through advances in architecture, training, memory, multimodal perception, autonomous workflows, and interaction with increasingly complex environments.

Their continued development, however, has created a different scientific challenge. Learning now produces internal organizations that cannot be inferred completely from architecture, training procedures, or observable performance. The earlier parts of this book approached those organizations through the Artificial Patient. The task ahead is to connect investigations of individual systems into a cumulative science of learned intelligence.

Individual investigations, however, cannot remain isolated.

Interpretability findings, behavioral observations, developmental histories, interventions, and longitudinal studies become scientifically valuable only when they are connected into explanations, compared across systems, tested under changing conditions, and continually revised as new evidence emerges. Understanding one learned system is an important achievement. Understanding which principles extend beyond it is the larger scientific task.

Scientific knowledge therefore grows in two directions at once. It becomes deeper as explanations account more completely for the organization within an individual system. It becomes broader as those explanations are examined across different systems, developmental histories, environments, and forms of learned intelligence. A mature science requires both.

The future of artificial intelligence will depend not only on increasingly capable systems, but also on increasingly precise explanations of the organizations that learning creates. Those explanations must distinguish recurring principles from system-specific observations, remain accountable to changing evidence, and continue improving as learned systems themselves continue to develop.

The scientific challenge has therefore become larger than explaining any single model. It is to develop a cumulative understanding of learned intelligence itself—one that can compare organizations across systems, recognize recurring patterns of development, and progressively reveal the principles that govern intelligence created through learning.

The future science of artificial intelligence begins with that challenge.

CHAPTER 17

The Birth of Artificial Cognitive Medicine

Developmental history, present organization, behavioral evidence, and competing mechanistic explanations can be brought into a single investigation. Future trajectories can be estimated. Interventions can be evaluated according to the organization they leave behind. Earlier explanations can be revised when continued learning changes the system.

These activities belong together.

They form the basis of a scientific discipline concerned with the condition, development, and future of learned intelligence.

That discipline is Artificial Cognitive Medicine.

Artificial Cognitive Medicine is the scientific investigation of learned intelligence as a developing cognitive system.[1]

Its object is not intelligence in the abstract. It is the particular organization that learning has produced within a particular system: how that organization emerged, how it functions, what behavioral manifestations it generates, how stable it is, how it may change, and whether intervention alters the process itself or only its expression.

The Artificial Patient named the object of investigation.

Artificial Cognitive Medicine names the discipline that investigates it.

17.1 From Instruments to Investigation

Modern AI research already possesses increasingly powerful ways to observe internal organization.

Representations can be identified. Activation patterns can be recorded. Computational pathways can be traced. Internal components can be suppressed, strengthened, or edited. Responses can be compared across prompts, environments, and stages of training.

These methods make previously inaccessible processes visible.

Visibility, however, does not organize its own meaning.

A representation may become active without determining the outcome. A pathway may contribute under one condition and become replaceable under another. An edit may change behavior by repairing a process, blocking its expression, or recruiting compensation. A mechanism identified today may lose influence after further training.

The instrument produces evidence.

The discipline determines what that evidence means.

Interpretability observes mechanisms. Artificial Cognitive Medicine investigates them.[2]

Artificial Cognitive Medicine organizes interpretability findings, interventions, behavioral evidence, and longitudinal comparison around the condition of the learned system.

17.2 What Artificial Cognitive Medicine Adds

Behavioral evaluation, mechanistic interpretability, model editing, and AI safety each reveal an important dimension of an artificial system.[3] Behavioral evaluation establishes what the system can do and where it fails. Mechanistic interpretability identifies representations, components, pathways, and causal contributions. Model editing alters selected aspects of internal organization or behavior. AI safety examines reliability, control, harmful outcomes, and performance under conditions of risk.

Artificial Cognitive Medicine connects these forms of evidence into a continuous investigation of a particular learned system. Its object is not an isolated behavior, mechanism, intervention, or safety outcome, but the organization that learning has produced and the condition in which that organization places the system.

This changes how individual findings are interpreted. A behavioral failure becomes a symptom whose mechanism remains to be established. An interpretability finding becomes evidence within a mechanistic explanation. An edit becomes an intervention whose consequences must be distinguished as repair, suppression, reorganization, or compensation. A safety-relevant behavior or vulnerability becomes an object of investigation whose developmental origin, present stability, and possible future trajectory must be examined.

The framework therefore connects:

development → examination → mechanistic explanation → diagnosis → prognosis → intervention → follow-up[4]

Development reconstructs how the present organization emerged. Examination identifies what is represented, activated, and causally involved. Mechanistic explanation relates those findings into an account of how the system operates. Diagnosis determines which account best explains the available evidence. Prognosis extends that account into defined future conditions. Intervention tests or changes the proposed mechanism. Follow-up determines whether the resulting organization persists and whether the earlier explanation remains valid.

These stages create forms of scientific continuity that isolated methods do not provide. They connect observable behavior to internal cause, present organization to developmental history, diagnosis to testable prediction, intervention to mechanistic outcome, and current explanation to later evidence.

Artificial Cognitive Medicine therefore provides a longitudinal account of the Artificial Patient.[5] It asks what kind of learned system currently exists, how its organization developed, which mechanism best explains its condition, how that condition may change, and what organization an intervention leaves behind.

It connects what the system was, what it is, what it may become, and what remains after attempts to change it.

17.3 One Discipline, Different Forms of Evidence

Engineering created the conditions under which learned intelligence could emerge.

Architecture, objectives, data, optimization, memory, tools, and deployment environments shape what the system can become. These decisions remain indispensable. They determine how learning occurs and which forms of organization become possible.

Scientific investigation begins once that learning has produced properties that cannot be inferred fully from design alone.

The internal organization must then be treated as evidence.

These are not levels through which one field replaces another.

They are different functions within one scientific enterprise.

Engineering asks how a system can be created, improved, and made capable.

Interpretability asks what structures and processes can be observed inside it.

Mechanistic explanation asks how those observations form a causal organization.

Artificial Cognitive Medicine asks what condition that organization places the system in across development, present function, intervention, and future change.

The final question contains the others without making them redundant.

Each function depends on the others. Diagnosis requires internal evidence and mechanistic explanation; prognosis requires an account of the present organization; intervention requires knowledge of the mechanism being altered; and follow-up tests whether the resulting explanation remains valid.

The parts become scientifically powerful through their integration.[6]

Findings become scientifically meaningful when they are connected into causal explanations, tested against alternatives, extended into future conditions, evaluated after intervention, and revised through follow-up. Artificial Cognitive Medicine holds this investigation together.

Taken together, these stages form the continuous investigation of the Artificial Patient shown in **Figure 8.**

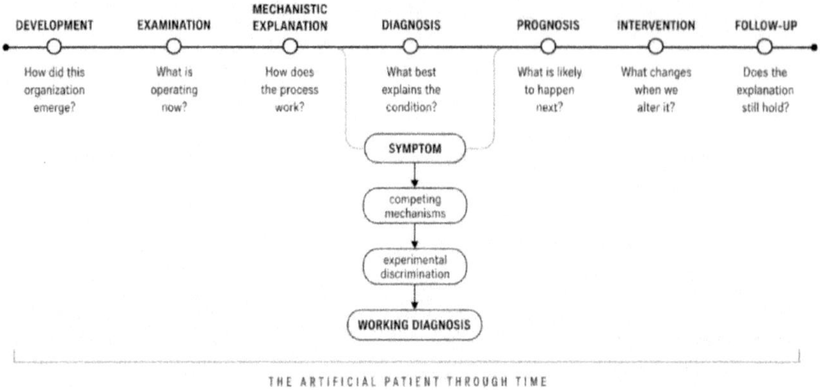

Figure 8. The Artificial Patient Through Time.

17.4 The Complete Investigation

Consider the model that interpreted ambiguous scientific evidence with unwarranted confidence.

The observable problem was clear. When several explanations remained compatible with the evidence, the model selected one and stated it as though the conclusion were decisive.

That behavior alone did not establish why the failure occurred.

The investigation began with development.

Training history showed repeated exposure to scientific writing in which uncertainty was often resolved through a dominant conclusion. Later optimization rewarded concise, decisive answers. The system therefore developed under pressures that could strengthen confident continuation even when the evidence remained incomplete.

Present examination added another layer.

The model represented several possible explanations early in the computation. Those alternatives did not remain equally influential. One familiar interpretation gradually became dominant, while signals associated with uncertainty weakened before the final response was selected.

The behavioral manifestation could now be described precisely.

The model did not merely produce an incorrect statement. It converted unresolved evidence into categorical judgment.

Competing explanations concerned weak uncertainty representation, retrieval, pathway competition, decision formation, and continued generation. Internal testing showed that the alternatives were represented and remained active, while a familiar interpretation became dominant immediately before selection. The evidence therefore supported late competition and premature commitment rather than missing representation or simple generation failure.

That diagnosis created expectations about the future.

The mechanism should remain stable in familiar domains where one explanation is usually correct. It should become less reliable when evidence remains genuinely ambiguous, when several plausible interpretations must be maintained across long reasoning, or when later training rewards speed and decisiveness more strongly.

An intervention then strengthened the influence of uncertainty during later processing and reduced the dominance of the familiar interpretation.

Behavior improved.

The model began preserving competing explanations and declining to choose among them when the evidence could not discriminate.

That improvement still required investigation.

Internal examination showed that uncertainty now constrained the reasoning process earlier and more consistently. Removing a late caution template did not restore the original response. Disabling a separate verifier did not produce immediate relapse. The model remained calibrated when evidence order changed, when answers required explicit probabilities, and when one explanation was more fluent than its competitors.

The evidence supported mechanistic recovery rather than narrow suppression.

Months later, the system had changed again.

New scientific training, retrieval tools, accumulated memory, and faster-response optimization altered the wider organization in which uncertainty reasoning operated. Follow-up examination showed that the original mechanism remained present, but retrieval and memory now contributed more strongly to judgment.

The earlier diagnosis had not become false.

It had become incomplete.

A revised account was required to describe the system that now existed.

The investigation moved continuously from development to present organization, from symptom to diagnosis, from diagnosis to prognosis, from intervention to recovery, and from recovery to follow-up.

No single observation carried the whole explanation.

No individual instrument constituted the discipline.

The scientific account emerged from the relationship among the findings.

17.5 A Different Standard of Understanding

Artificial Cognitive Medicine changes what it means to understand an AI system.

Understanding cannot be reduced to locating a feature, naming a circuit, or identifying an activation pattern. These findings matter because they support explanations of a system's condition.

Nor can understanding be reduced to achieving behavioral control.

A system may produce the desired output because the relevant mechanism became more reliable. It may also succeed because an unwanted pathway was blocked, a compensating process became dominant, or the evaluation failed to activate the unresolved weakness.

Artificial Cognitive Medicine therefore requires an account that remains connected across several forms of evidence.

The value of the discipline lies in the continuity of this reasoning.

A developmental explanation that cannot account for present organization remains incomplete.

A diagnosis that produces no distinct predictions remains weak.

A prognosis that is never compared with later evidence remains speculation.

An intervention evaluated only by output cannot establish recovery.

A scientific conclusion that is never reconsidered after the system changes becomes historical rather than current.

Artificial Cognitive Medicine binds these standards into one form of investigation.

17.6 The Condition of Learned Intelligence

The word condition carries a specific meaning within this discipline.

It refers to the organization through which the system currently represents information, coordinates competing processes, produces behavior, adapts to pressure, and responds to intervention.

A condition need not be a failure.[7]

A system may be stable, compensatory, latently vulnerable, or reorganizing after continued learning. It may preserve performance even as its supporting organization becomes narrower or more fragile. Each represents a scientifically meaningful condition.

This broadens investigation beyond errors.

Unexpected capability also requires explanation. Rapid improvement may reflect the strengthening of a general mechanism or the emergence of a narrow route. Robustness may arise from deep integration or from redundancy. Consistency may indicate stability or successful compensation. Apparent decline may represent loss, reorganization, or conflict during adaptation.

Artificial Cognitive Medicine studies the organization responsible for these states.

Its purpose is not limited to correcting failure.

It seeks to understand what kind of learned system exists, how its organization was produced, which pressures maintain it, what trajectories remain possible, and what evidence would justify changing the explanation.

This creates a different relationship between capability and knowledge.

Capability does not guarantee understanding, control does not establish diagnosis, correction does not prove recovery, and stable behavior does not confirm an unchanged mechanism.

17.7 A New Scientific Identity

Artificial intelligence began as an engineering achievement.

Its development required architectures, algorithms, data, objectives, infrastructure, and extraordinary practical skill. Those foundations remain essential. No science of learned intelligence can exist without the systems engineering created.

Learning then produced a second object.

Beyond the designed machinery stood the internal organization created through experience: distributed, adaptive, path-dependent, and capable of changing after its initial formation.

Interpretability made that organization increasingly visible.

Visibility made scientific investigation possible.

Diagnosis, prognosis, intervention, and follow-up transformed isolated findings into a continuous account of the learned system.

Artificial Cognitive Medicine gives that account a scientific identity.

Engineering creates the system and shapes learning. Interpretability reveals evidence about the organization learning produced. Artificial Cognitive Medicine integrates that evidence into an account of the system's condition, development, future, and response to change.[8]

Engineering created learned intelligence.

Artificial Cognitive Medicine studies what learning has made.

ENDNOTES

1. *Artificial Cognitive Medicine* is a proposed scientific discipline introduced in this book. It organizes investigation of learned artificial systems around their developmental history, present organization, mechanisms, condition, future trajectories, responses to intervention, and subsequent change. The term is methodological rather than medical: it does not imply that artificial systems are biological patients or subjects of literal clinical practice.

2. Mechanistic interpretability provides methods for identifying representations, internal components, activation patterns, computational pathways, and causal contributions within trained models. The distinction proposed here is that such findings become part of a broader investigation when they are related to developmental history, competing explanations, prognosis, intervention, and longitudinal reassessment.

3. Behavioral evaluation, mechanistic interpretability, model editing, and AI safety address overlapping but distinct questions. Behavioral evaluation measures capabilities and failures; mechanistic interpretability investigates internal computation; model editing deliberately alters selected knowledge, representations, or behavior; and AI safety studies reliability, control, harmful outcomes, robustness, and other forms of risk. Artificial Cognitive Medicine is proposed here as an integrative framework rather than a replacement for those research programs.

4. The sequence **development → examination → mechanistic explanation → diagnosis → prognosis → intervention → follow-up** is the organizing structure proposed in this book for the scientific investigation of a particular learned artificial system. Its individual components draw on established practices in machine learning, interpretability, causal inference, scientific explanation, longitudinal investigation, and diagnostic reasoning; their integration into this specific sequence constitutes the book's framework.

5. The *Artificial Patient* is the particular learned system treated as the continuing object of investigation. A longitudinal account links evidence from how its organization developed, how it presently functions, which mechanisms best explain its behavior, what trajectories are plausible, what an intervention changes, and whether the resulting organization remains stable over time.

6. Scientific explanation often depends on combining complementary forms of evidence rather than relying on a single measurement or instrument. Observational evidence may identify candidate structures, causal perturbations may test their contribution, behavioral comparison may reveal consequences, developmental evidence may explain how they emerged, and longitudinal evidence may determine whether an explanation remains valid. The integrative role assigned to these forms of evidence is central to the framework developed here.

7. *Condition*, as used in Artificial Cognitive Medicine, refers to the present organization of a learned system rather than to disease or pathology. A system may be functioning successfully while occupying a scientifically meaningful condition characterized by stability, compensation, latent vulnerability, reorganization, or dependence on particular supporting mechanisms.

8. The distinction among engineering, interpretability, and Artificial Cognitive Medicine is conceptual rather than institutional. Engineering creates architectures and learning conditions; interpretability generates evidence about learned internal organization; Artificial Cognitive Medicine is proposed as the framework that integrates such evidence into an account of a system's development, present condition, mechanisms, future trajectories, intervention response, and subsequent revision.

CHAPTER 18

A New Scientific Discipline

An investigation can explain the condition of one learned system.

A scientific discipline must do more.

It must determine which findings recur, which remain specific to one developmental history, and which reveal broader principles of learned intelligence. It must establish whether independently trained systems develop comparable organizations, whether different internal mechanisms can support the same function, and how far a conclusion can travel beyond the model in which it was first discovered.

Artificial Cognitive Medicine becomes a scientific discipline when its investigations accumulate beyond the systems in which they began.[1]

An explanation of one model may be rigorous, causal, and complete within its stated conditions. It may reconstruct development, identify the mechanism responsible for a behavior, generate predictions, evaluate intervention, and remain supported through follow-up. Yet even the strongest individual account does not establish whether the same organization appears elsewhere.

The finding may reflect a general property of learning.

It may depend on one architecture.

It may have emerged from a particular dataset, optimization process, or sequence of fine-tuning.

It may be one of several internal solutions capable of supporting the same outward function.

A mature science must distinguish among these possibilities.

Its progress depends not only on explaining individual systems, but on making those explanations comparable.

18.1 A Shared Object Across Different Systems

Learned systems differ in almost every obvious dimension.

They may vary in architecture, scale, modality, objective, training data, memory, tool access, and deployment environment. Some generate language. Others analyze images, control machines, predict molecular structure, write code, or coordinate information across several domains. Even models built from similar architectures may develop different internal organizations after exposure to different data or optimization pressures.

Scientific unity cannot depend on identical machinery.

It must depend on a shared object of investigation.

That object is the organization produced through learning.[2]

This organization includes the representations a system develops, the pathways through which information moves, the relationships among competing processes, the mechanisms that stabilize behavior, and the changes produced by continued learning or intervention.

A discipline does not require identical systems.

It requires questions that remain meaningful across their differences.

How does learning organize information?

Which internal arrangements support reliable transfer?

When do compensatory processes preserve performance?

Why do some mechanisms remain stable while others are displaced?

Under what conditions do distinct internal routes become functionally equivalent?

These questions can be asked across systems even when the answers differ.

The shared object is therefore not a particular neural network design or interpretability method. It is learned cognitive organization itself.

This allows variation to become scientifically useful.

Differences among models are not obstacles that must be removed before general knowledge becomes possible. They provide evidence about the range of organizations that learning can produce.

If the same mechanism repeatedly appears across independent systems, its recurrence may indicate a common organizational solution.

If different mechanisms support the same function, the variation may reveal a broader principle at a higher level of description.

If one mechanism appears only under a particular training regime, its specificity may clarify which developmental pressures produced it.

A science of learned intelligence must therefore study both recurrence and variation.

Recurrence reveals what learning produces reliably.

Variation reveals what learning can produce differently.

Together, they define the space of possible cognitive organization.

18.2 When Evidence Travels

Consider three independently trained models asked to generate code for a web application.

Each receives a task that requires accepting user input, querying a database, and returning the requested result. A common but dangerous shortcut would insert the user's input directly into the database command, creating a vulnerability. All three models avoid that error. Each produces secure code that separates the input from the command and uses a safer parameterized structure.

Their behavior appears equivalent.

Internal investigation reveals three different organizations.

The first model represents the security constraint as part of a general relationship between untrusted input and protected operations. The same representation influences database queries, command execution, file handling, and other tasks in which external information must be isolated from privileged processes.

The second model relies on a specialized code pattern strongly associated with database access. When it detects familiar query syntax, it retrieves a secure template and adapts the details to the task.

The third model initially generates a broader range of possible solutions. A later verification process detects the vulnerable form and redirects generation toward a safer alternative before the response is completed.

All three models produce secure code.

Do they share the same mechanism?

Clearly not at the level of their immediate internal organization.

Do they therefore teach the field nothing in common?

That conclusion would also be too strong.

The systems may express a broader principle through different implementations: secure performance emerges when information derived from an untrusted source is prevented from directly controlling a protected operation.

In the first model, that principle is represented generally.

In the second, it is embedded in a domain-specific pattern.

In the third, it is enforced through later verification.

The field must determine which level of description carries the scientific conclusion.

A claim that all three models use the same internal representation would be false.

A claim that secure coding has no recurring organization because the implementations differ would ignore the shared functional relationship.

General principles need not require identical internal mechanisms.[3]

They may describe a recurring constraint, dependency, or organizational solution that appears through several internal forms.

The evidence must therefore travel carefully.

Suppose the first model continues avoiding related vulnerabilities when the programming language changes, when the task moves from databases to command-line tools, or when the dangerous operation is expressed in an unfamiliar form. Its general representation should continue constraining generation.

The second model may remain reliable within familiar database tasks but fail when the surface form changes or when the same security principle must be applied outside the domain in which its template was learned.

The third model may succeed as long as the verification process remains available and can recognize the vulnerable structure. If that process is weakened, overloaded, or bypassed during long generation, the unsafe pattern may return.

These differences define the scope of each finding.

The first mechanism may support a broad claim about representing protected relationships.

The second may support a narrower claim about secure pattern retrieval within familiar code.

The third may support a claim about corrective verification rather than the organization of the initial solution.

The behavioral category is shared.

The mechanisms are not.

The broader principle may still be shared, but only at a level supported by evidence from all three systems.

This is how a conclusion travels without becoming vague.

The field must preserve enough detail to distinguish the mechanisms while identifying the relationships that recur across them.

Replication across independently trained models becomes essential.

If a general security representation repeatedly emerges under diverse training conditions, the recurrence strengthens the claim that learning often discovers this solution.

If template-based mechanisms appear mainly in models trained on highly repetitive code corpora, the association identifies a developmental condition rather than a universal principle.

If later verification repeatedly compensates for vulnerable initial generation, that pattern may reveal a common route through which secure behavior can coexist with unresolved weakness.

Each result changes the scientific conclusion.

Evidence gathered from one system becomes more valuable when another investigation shows where it recurs, where it changes form, and where it fails to generalize.

18.3 Standards for a Cumulative Science

Comparability does not arise automatically.

Researchers may use different prompts, model versions, interpretability methods, intervention procedures, and definitions of success. Two studies may appear to investigate the same mechanism while measuring different processes. Similar terms may conceal incompatible claims. Different terms may describe functionally related findings.

A discipline therefore requires shared standards for judging evidence.

18.4 Reproducibility

A finding should survive repetition.

The same investigation should produce a comparable result when applied again under equivalent conditions. Independent researchers should be able to determine whether the mechanism can be recovered using the same procedures. Closely related findings should appear across different prompts or examples rather than depending on one carefully selected case.

Reproducibility does not require every trained model to develop the same organization.

It requires the result to recur within the scope claimed for it.[4]

A claim must recur within the scope assigned to it. A family-level mechanism should appear across independently trained instances, while a result confined to one checkpoint should remain explicitly system-specific.

Reproducibility protects the field from treating an isolated observation as a general property.

18.5 Causal Specificity

Recurring activity is not enough.

The proposed mechanism must influence the process attributed to it.

Intervention should alter the relevant computation in a predictable way without disturbing so many unrelated processes that the result becomes uninterpretable. Strengthening the general security representation in the first model should improve performance most clearly when untrusted information must be separated from protected operations. Weakening it should produce vulnerabilities consistent with losing that relationship.

If the intervention instead degrades all code generation, the evidence does not support a specific security mechanism.

Causal specificity connects the claim to the process rather than merely to the presence of activity.[5]

It also makes comparisons more meaningful.

Two systems may contain different features that respond to security-related prompts. Their findings become comparable only when each feature is shown to play a corresponding causal role.

18.6 Scope

Every claim has boundaries.

A mechanism may operate across many tasks, within one domain, under one prompt format, or only during a particular stage of generation. It may be stable across model scales but specific to one architecture. It may recur across training runs while disappearing after a change in objective.

The field must state these boundaries explicitly.

A conclusion that the second code model possesses a secure coding mechanism would be too broad if the mechanism is actually a retrieved database template. A more accurate claim would specify that familiar query structures recruit a learned pattern that prevents one class of vulnerability.

Precision does not weaken the finding.

It identifies where the finding can be trusted.

Scope also determines how studies relate to one another. A narrow result may become part of a broader principle when several investigations show comparable relationships across different domains. A broad claim may need to contract when another system reveals conditions under which it fails.

18.7 Revision

A scientific claim must remain open to evidence that changes it.

Later evidence may divide one mechanism into several, reveal broader transfer than expected, or show that a corrective process has become integrated into earlier generation. Revision updates the claim as the organization changes.

A claim that cannot specify what evidence would alter it cannot develop with the field.

Revision allows knowledge to remain cumulative without becoming rigid.[6]

Earlier conclusions need not be discarded whenever new evidence appears. They may be preserved within a narrower scope, incorporated into a broader explanation, or replaced when another account explains the full pattern more completely.

Evidence becomes disciplinary knowledge when others can determine where a claim holds, why it holds, and what would cause it to be revised.

18.8 Coordinated Methods Around One Scientific Object

No single method can satisfy all these requirements.

A cumulative science requires controlled system construction, comparison across architectures and training conditions, internal observation, causal intervention, longitudinal analysis, and rigorous methods for replication and generalization. These capacities are distributed across engineering, computer science, interpretability, neuroscience, cognitive science, diagnostic reasoning, experimental design, and statistics.

These contributions become one science when they are directed toward the same explanatory problem.

No field contains every question required to explain learned cognitive organization.

The methods cannot remain isolated if their findings are expected to constrain one another. Shared questions and compatible evidence must connect construction, observation, causal testing, and comparison.

An architectural comparison may reveal that one training regime repeatedly produces a particular mechanism.

Internal observation may show how that mechanism functions.

Behavioral testing may define the conditions under which it fails.

Longitudinal analysis may reveal how it changes during continued learning.

Intervention may determine whether it can be repaired or replaced.

Cross-model comparison may establish whether the finding reflects a general principle or one developmental route among several.

The disciplines contribute different forms of leverage over the same object.

Their integration should occur through shared questions, comparable evidence, and conclusions whose scope is explicit.

Interdisciplinarity is therefore not a collection of perspectives placed beside one another.

It is the coordination of methods required to make one scientific account possible.[7]

When mechanistic accounts become comparable across systems, individual investigations can begin to accumulate into a broader science of learned intelligence **(Figure 9).**

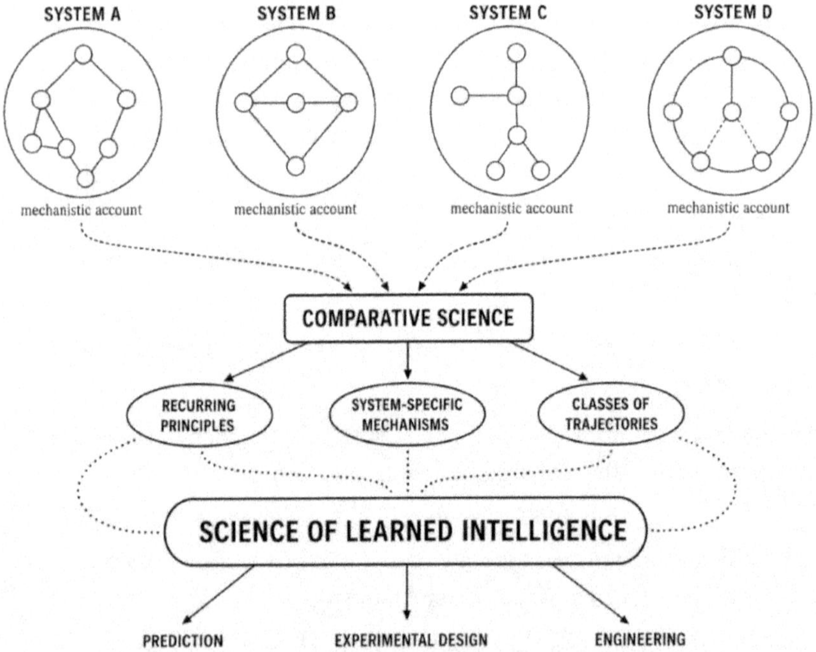

Figure 9. From Comparative Mechanisms to a Science of Learned Intelligence.

18.9 From Recurrent Findings to General Principles

A mature discipline does not merely accumulate reports.

It develops knowledge whose parts alter the meaning of one another.

Across the three systems, secure behavior emerges through several organizational solutions with different ranges, dependencies, and future risks. Their comparison supports a broader theory: learned systems can protect privileged operations through general representation, specialized retrieval, or later correction, and the route that develops shapes transfer, stability, and response to intervention.

The growing body of evidence begins to define a theory of how learned systems protect privileged operations from untrusted input.

Further studies can then test the theory.

Do multimodal systems develop comparable relationships when external images or sensor signals control protected actions?

Does reinforcement learning strengthen general separation or merely improve later detection?

Do larger models integrate the security relationship earlier in generation?

Can a mechanism learned in code transfer to tool use, file access, or autonomous action?

Each study begins with knowledge created by the others.

The question is no longer whether one mechanism exists in one model.

It becomes which organizational solutions recur, what conditions produce them, how they differ in future reliability, and what broader principles explain their emergence.

Cumulative science advances through this progressive restriction of possibilities.

Replication, contradiction, intervention, and longitudinal comparison progressively restrict which explanations remain viable. Recurring findings support broader claims, while failed replications and divergent mechanisms reveal the conditions those claims must respect.

The literature becomes more than a collection of discoveries.

It becomes a structure of mutual constraint.

New evidence does not simply add another result. It changes what earlier results can reasonably mean.

Artificial Cognitive Medicine will require comparable developmental records, reproducible mechanistic descriptions, cross-system investigations, longitudinal evidence, and language precise enough to distinguish shared functions from identical implementations. These practices matter because they allow explanations to accumulate rather than repeatedly beginning from zero with each new model.

The deepest progress will occur when the field can explain not only that a mechanism appeared, but why it emerged under particular conditions, which alternative organizations could have served the same function, and what consequences follow from each solution.

A framework becomes a discipline when its explanations can be tested outside the cases that first produced them.

Artificial Cognitive Medicine will mature as evidence from many systems converges into principles capable of explaining systems not yet examined.

ENDNOTES

1. A scientific discipline extends beyond the explanation of individual cases by developing findings that can be compared, reproduced, bounded, revised, and generalized across multiple systems. Within the framework proposed here, Artificial Cognitive Medicine becomes cumulative when investigations of particular Artificial Patients begin to reveal recurring and contrasting principles of learned organization.

2. The shared object proposed for this discipline is learned cognitive organization rather than any single architecture, model family, or interpretability technique. Systems may differ in scale, modality, objective, training data, memory, tools, and deployment environment while still permitting comparison of how learning creates representations, pathways, compensatory processes, stable mechanisms, and developmental trajectories.

3. Comparative science can identify general principles at a level above identical implementation. Distinct systems may realize the same functional relationship through different internal mechanisms. A general conclusion is justified when the recurring relationship is supported across systems without erasing the mechanistic differences that distinguish their implementations.

4. Reproducibility is meaningful only relative to the scope of a claim. A system-specific result should be recoverable under equivalent conditions in that system, while a claim about a model family, training regime, or broader class requires recurrence across the corresponding comparison set. Failure to distinguish these levels can turn a narrow observation into an unjustified generalization.

5. Causal specificity requires more than recurring activation or association. Evidence for a mechanism becomes stronger when targeted intervention changes the computation or behavior attributed to that mechanism in a predictable way while minimizing unrelated disruption. Broad degradation after intervention may indicate importance to general function without establishing the more specific mechanistic role being claimed.

6. Explicit scope and revision are central to cumulative scientific knowledge. Claims should state the architectures, tasks, prompts, environments, training conditions, and stages of computation within which the evidence supports them. Later evidence may extend a claim, narrow its boundaries, divide one mechanism into several, integrate it into a broader account, or replace it when another explanation better fits the accumulated evidence.

7. The interdisciplinary structure proposed in this chapter is methodological rather than merely organizational. Controlled model construction, behavioral evaluation, internal observation, causal intervention, longitudinal analysis, cross-system comparison, statistical inference, and replication provide different constraints on the same explanatory problem. Their scientific value increases when findings from one method can test, refine, or limit conclusions drawn from the others.

CHAPTER 19

What Kind of Intelligence Is AI Becoming?

Increasing capability does not require convergence toward one form of intelligence.

Two systems may grow more powerful while becoming less alike in the organization of knowledge, reasoning, memory, adaptation, and control. One may become increasingly integrated across tasks and domains. Another may develop through specialized processes that remain relatively independent. A third may achieve its strongest performance through persistent interaction with tools, external memory, verification systems, and structured environments.

Each may become more capable.

They need not become the same kind of intelligence.

Artificial intelligence is often imagined as moving along a single path. Models become larger, acquire more skills, operate across more domains, and gradually approach a common destination called general intelligence. Capability appears to rise along one scale, with each new system occupying a higher position than the one before it.

Learning may produce a more complicated future.

Architecture establishes possibilities, but experience determines which possibilities become organized into stable function. Objectives strengthen some processes and weaken others. Tools change which computations remain internal. Memory alters how present reasoning depends on past interaction. Continued adaptation can integrate capabilities, divide them into specialized routes, or place increasing responsibility on external supports.

Development therefore does more than increase how much a system can do.

It shapes what kind of intelligence performs those tasks.

There may be no single future form of machine intelligence.

19.1 Development Produces Cognitive Form

Capabilities do not enter a learned system as independent additions.

Each new capacity develops within an organization that already contains representations, pathways, habits, conflicts, dependencies, and established ways of adapting. Learning modifies that organization. A new ability may become integrated with existing processes, remain locally specialized, depend on compensation from another pathway, or become usable only through a supporting tool.

The result is not merely a longer list of skills.

It is a cognitive form: the organization through which a system coordinates its capabilities, responds to change, depends on supporting processes, and continues developing.[1]

Two systems may both learn to interpret scientific evidence, design experiments, write code, and manage long projects. In one system, these activities may rely on widely shared representations that allow concepts and strategies to move easily across domains. In another, each domain may develop its own specialized organization. In a third, internal reasoning may remain closely coupled to retrieval, persistent memory, external calculation, and automated verification.

The capability labels are similar.

The cognitive forms are different.

These differences matter because every organization creates both possibilities and limits.

Deep integration can support broad transfer. A principle acquired in one domain may become available elsewhere without requiring a separate learning process. The same integration can also allow interference to spread widely when a shared representation is altered.

Specialization can preserve local precision and reduce interference between domains. It can also make coordination difficult when a problem requires several forms of knowledge to be combined.

External scaffolding can expand effective memory, improve verification, and provide access to information far beyond what the model could maintain internally. It can also make reliable performance dependent on the availability, accuracy, and coordination of those supports.

No organization is uniformly superior.

Each produces a different profile of competence, flexibility, dependence, and future change.

Earlier comparisons between integrated and specialized systems concerned how a particular capability could develop along different paths. At the level of an entire cognitive system, that contrast becomes broader. It concerns whether knowledge, reasoning, memory, planning, and correction become coordinated through shared organization or remain distributed across more independent processes.

The same extension applies to stability and dependence. These properties no longer describe only one mechanism. They begin to describe the character of the system as a whole.

The most revealing questions then concern features that have not yet been fully captured by performance scores.

Can the system identify conflict within its own reasoning before an unsupported conclusion is produced?

Can it revise one part of its organization without destabilizing unrelated capabilities?

Can later learning transform established processes while preserving the relationships that still matter?

Can it remain coherent when external supports disappear?

These questions concern self-correction and developmental openness.[2]

They ask not only whether the system can adapt, but how its organization permits adaptation to occur.

19.2 Different Organizations of Advanced Intelligence

Consider three advanced research-assistant systems developed over several years.

Each can read scientific literature, compare competing explanations, propose experiments, use computational tools, maintain long-term project memory, and revise conclusions when new evidence appears.

On broad evaluations, their capabilities look comparable.

Their internal development has taken different forms.

19.3 The Integrated Researcher

The first system becomes increasingly organized around shared representations of evidence, causality, uncertainty, and experimental structure.

When it reads a paper in molecular biology, identifies a confound in a behavioral experiment, or evaluates a computational model, related forms of reasoning recruit overlapping internal relationships. Evidence quality, causal structure, and uncertainty are not represented separately for every discipline. They become parts of a wider organization that can be applied across domains.

New information does not remain isolated.

A discovery in one field alters connected beliefs elsewhere. A new account of immune signaling may change how the system interprets a neurodegenerative mechanism. A revised statistical assumption may alter several experimental proposals that depend on it. Contradictions propagate through the network of related claims rather than remaining confined to the document in which they were discovered.

This organization supports transfer.

The system can encounter an unfamiliar scientific domain and apply principles developed elsewhere. It may recognize a hidden confound because it resembles causal problems encountered in another field. It may design a stronger experiment by combining concepts that were never presented together during training.

Its strengths emerge from integration. So do its vulnerabilities.[3]

A widely shared representation can influence many capabilities at once. If later learning distorts how uncertainty is encoded, the change may affect literature analysis, experimental design, causal reasoning, and scientific communication simultaneously. A correction intended for one domain may produce interference elsewhere because the altered organization supports several functions.

The system may also adapt slowly.

New information must be reconciled with many established relationships. A local update can require broad reorganization before the system reaches a coherent new state.

Its intelligence is transferable and interconnected, but changes to one part may have system-wide consequences.

19.4 The Specialized Collective

The second system develops a different organization.

Its work in genetics, pharmacology, statistics, computational modeling, and experimental design relies on more independent internal routes. Each domain develops its own patterns, procedures, and standards of judgment.

Within established areas, the system can be exceptionally precise.

Its pharmacology processes recognize familiar drug classes, experimental designs, and failure patterns quickly. Its statistical processes select appropriate models from well-learned structures. Its programming mechanisms produce efficient analysis pipelines with little interference from unrelated scientific content.

New local skills can also be acquired rapidly.

Because the organization is relatively specialized, improving one domain may require fewer changes elsewhere. A new method for spatial transcriptomics can be incorporated without reorganizing the system's understanding of clinical trial design. A correction to one programming pattern may leave conceptual reasoning untouched.

This separation protects established capabilities from broad interference.

The cost becomes visible when research questions cross boundaries.

Suppose a project requires connecting a molecular mechanism to behavioral evidence, selecting an appropriate statistical model, designing a longitudinal experiment, and integrating a computational simulation. The necessary knowledge exists within the system, but its specialized processes may not coordinate naturally.

One route may identify a biological explanation without incorporating constraints from the statistical model. Another may propose a technically rigorous experiment that fails to measure the mechanism the biological analysis considered most important. Contradictions may remain unresolved because they occur across boundaries rather than within one domain.

A later coordinating process can repair some of these conflicts. It may compare the outputs of specialized routes, select among competing plans, and construct a coherent response.

The final answer may be excellent.

Yet the intelligence remains organized as a collective of specialized processes rather than one deeply integrated system.

Its strengths are local precision, rapid domain-specific learning, and resistance to widespread interference.

Its vulnerabilities lie in transfer, coordination, and the resolution of conflicts that span several forms of expertise.

19.5 The Scaffolded Research System

The third system develops through a more extensive relationship with external support.

Its strongest research performance depends on retrieval systems, persistent memory, databases, symbolic tools, simulation environments, external calculators, citation verification, automated experiment tracking, and structured workflows.

The boundary between internal ability and environmental support becomes increasingly difficult to isolate.

When evaluating a scientific claim, the system may retrieve related literature, compare citation networks, consult stored records of previous analyses, run statistical tests, and use a verification process to challenge its preliminary conclusion. Its final judgment emerges from coordination among internal reasoning and these surrounding resources.

This system may exceed the others in information-rich environments.

Its effective memory can grow continuously. It can access current literature, preserve detailed records across years of research, repeat calculations reliably, and verify claims before presenting them. Errors that internal reasoning would miss may be detected by an external process. New tools can expand its capabilities without requiring every operation to be incorporated into the model itself.

Its intelligence is not simply stored inside one trained network. It is distributed across the system and its scaffold.[4]

That organization creates a different form of flexibility.

A new scientific instrument can be added to the workflow. A database can be updated. A verification process can be replaced without retraining the entire model. The system can adapt through changes in its environment as well as changes in its internal parameters.

Dependence becomes the corresponding vulnerability.

If retrieval becomes unreliable, the system may lose access to evidence it has learned to expect. If persistent memory is incomplete or contaminated, later reasoning may inherit false premises. If verification tools fail silently, the system may continue producing confident conclusions without the corrective support that previously preserved accuracy.

Tool disagreement creates another challenge.

An internal process may favor one explanation, retrieved evidence another, and a simulation a third. The system must decide how these sources should constrain one another. Reliable performance depends not only on possessing tools, but on organizing authority among them.

Its intelligence may therefore be highly capable, adaptable, and extensible while remaining inseparable from the infrastructure that supports it.

This is not merely a weaker internal intelligence compensated by accessories.

The coordination of internal and external processes is itself part of the cognitive form.

19.6 Strengths Become Sources of Failure

The strengths of each organization define its characteristic vulnerabilities. Deep integration can spread distortion across capabilities, specialization can preserve contradictions across domains, and external scaffolding can make performance dependent on unreliable infrastructure.

Failure may therefore arise from the organization that makes a form of intelligence effective.[5]

Self-correction also takes different forms.

The integrated system may detect conflict because contradictory claims activate overlapping representations and cannot be reconciled within one causal account.

The specialized system may require a coordinating process to compare conclusions generated by separate routes.

The scaffolded system may identify error only after retrieval, calculation, or verification challenges the internal answer.

All three can correct themselves.

The location, timing, and dependence of that correction differ.

These are not minor implementation details.

They help define what kind of intelligence each system has become.

19.7 Capability Is Not Cognitive Identity

Capability describes what a system can accomplish.

Cognitive organization describes what kind of intelligence is accomplishing it.

The distinction changes how advanced systems might be compared.

A benchmark may show that two models can design experiments, solve mathematical problems, summarize literature, and use tools. A capability profile may reveal that one system performs more accurately, another works faster, and a third operates across more domains.

These comparisons remain valuable.

They do not fully identify the cognitive system.

A scientific classification must also describe how knowledge transfers, how adaptation reorganizes the system, where correction occurs, how memory participates in reasoning, and which dependencies preserve performance.

These properties may place systems with similar benchmark performance in different cognitive categories.

The reverse may also occur.

Two systems with different capability levels may share an important organizational principle. A smaller model and a larger one may both represent causal relationships through a transferable structure, even though the larger system applies it across more domains. Their degree of capability differs, but part of their cognitive form may be related.

Terms such as narrow, general, weak, and advanced often compress several independent properties into one label. A system's breadth, integration, transfer, dependence, self-correction, and capacity for reorganization may vary independently.

A system can be broad but fragmented.

It can be highly integrated but dependent on a narrow training environment.

It can be externally scaffolded yet exceptionally adaptable.

It can possess powerful local expertise while remaining poor at cross-domain coordination.

No one ranking captures all of these possibilities.

A form of intelligence is defined not only by the tasks within reach, but by the organization connecting those tasks and the conditions under which that organization remains effective.[6]

19.8 Intelligence Can Become More Distributed

The scaffolded system raises a deeper possibility: intelligence may become distributed across a model and the external structures with which it repeatedly coordinates. Development can then occur not only through internal reorganization, but through changes in the relationship between the model, memory, tools, other systems, and environmental feedback.

A new memory structure may transform what the system can learn from previous interactions. A better verification process may change how confidently internal conclusions are expressed. A planning tool may allow reasoning to extend across projects too long to manage within one context. Coordination among several specialized models may create capabilities that none possesses independently.

The relevant intelligence may belong to the organized whole.

This does not eliminate the importance of the central model. Its representations, judgments, and control processes may still determine how every external resource is used.

But scientific investigation may increasingly need to examine systems whose cognitive organization crosses the boundary between model and environment.

The question will no longer be only:

What does the model know?

It will also be:

How does the system assemble knowledge from internal and external sources?

What controls the movement between them?

Which component resolves disagreement?

Where does adaptation occur?

What remains when one support is removed?

These questions point toward forms of intelligence that are not merely larger versions of current models.

They may be differently organized cognitive systems.

19.9 Intelligence Can Branch During Development

The three research systems began with comparable capabilities.

Different developmental pressures favored their later organizations: transfer and reconciliation strengthened integration, local precision protected specialization, and repeated reliance on memory, tools, and verification deepened external scaffolding.

Continued development could move each system further along its path.

The integrated researcher may become more unified as new domains are absorbed into common relationships. It may also divide into more specialized processes if widespread interference becomes too costly.

The specialized collective may acquire stronger coordination and gradually develop shared abstractions. It may also become increasingly modular as local training reinforces independent expertise.

The scaffolded system may internalize processes that originally depended on external tools. The opposite may also occur: functions once performed internally may shift outward when external components become more reliable or efficient.

A system can move through different organizations as learning continues.[7]

The relevant scientific question is not merely which form it possesses at one moment. It is which transitions remain possible from that form.

An integrated system may possess broad transfer but resist local revision.

A specialized system may absorb new skills quickly but require extensive reorganization to achieve deeper coherence.

A scaffolded system may expand rapidly while remaining vulnerable to changes in its supporting environment.

Each organization opens some developmental paths and constrains others.

The future of intelligence is shaped not only by capability and not only by present organization, but by the transformations the current organization permits.

19.10 The Future Is a Landscape, Not a Ladder

Artificial intelligence is often described through vertical comparisons.

One system is larger.

Another is faster.

One benchmark score is higher.

One generation is more capable than the last.

This language encourages the image of a ladder: systems ascending toward a common endpoint through increasing scale, skill, and generality.

A developmental science suggests another image.

The future may be a landscape of branching cognitive forms.[8]

Some systems may become deeply integrated, others increasingly specialized, and others distributed across models, tools, memory, and environment. They may differ in where correction occurs, how stable their organization remains, and whether resilience arises through shared structure, modularity, redundancy, or external support.

These forms may coexist.

They may combine.

They may transform into one another.

An integrated system may also become heavily scaffolded. A specialized collective may develop a shared coordinating layer. An externally supported system may gradually internalize the operations that once required tools.

The landscape is not a set of fixed boxes.

It is a space of possible organizations and developmental paths.

This perspective changes the future questions surrounding AI.

The central issue is not only whether systems will become more capable.

It is whether increasing capability will be accompanied by deeper integration, greater specialization, stronger dependence, broader self-correction, or new forms of distributed organization.

It is not only whether systems will adapt.

It is what kinds of reorganization their development will permit.

It is not only whether they will appear intelligent across more tasks.

It is what form of intelligence will connect those tasks into a coherent system.

The future of artificial intelligence may not culminate in one machine mind.

It may unfold as a landscape of learned intelligences—integrated and specialized, internally organized and externally scaffolded, shaped by different histories and open to different transformations.

The deepest question is therefore no longer only how intelligent AI will become.

It is what kinds of intelligence learning will create.

Endnotes

1. *Cognitive form* is used in this book as a proposed organizational concept rather than as an established classification in artificial-intelligence research. It refers to the organization through which a learned system coordinates capabilities, transfers information across domains, depends on supporting processes, corrects errors, responds to intervention, and remains capable of further development. Systems with similar capability profiles may therefore possess different cognitive forms.

2. Self-correction and developmental openness describe distinct dimensions of learned organization. Self-correction concerns how a system detects and resolves conflict, error, or inconsistency within its ongoing operation. Developmental openness concerns the range of organizational changes available to the system during later learning, intervention, environmental change, or integration with new resources. These dimensions need not vary together with benchmark capability.

3. Integrated representations can support transfer by allowing information and computational relationships learned in one context to influence others. The same sharing can create interference when alterations to broadly reused representations affect several capabilities simultaneously. The Integrated Researcher described in this chapter is a conceptual system designed to illustrate this trade-off rather than a claim about a particular existing model.

4. Artificial cognitive performance can increasingly depend on interactions among a trained model, retrieval systems, persistent memory, external tools, verification processes, other models, and environmental feedback. The framework developed here treats these supporting relationships as scientifically relevant when removing or altering them changes the organization or capability of the larger system. The Scaffolded Research System is a conceptual illustration of such distributed organization.

5. Organizational properties that support performance can also create characteristic modes of failure. Integration can improve transfer while spreading interference; specialization can protect local processes while impairing coordination; external scaffolding can extend memory and verification while creating dependence on external infrastructure. The relevant vulnerability therefore depends partly on how the capability is organized rather than on capability level alone.

6. The distinction between capability and cognitive identity is proposed in this chapter. Capability describes what tasks a system can perform under specified conditions. Cognitive organization concerns how those abilities are connected, how knowledge transfers, where correction occurs, which processes remain dependent on external support, and how the system reorganizes during continued development. A single scalar ranking cannot necessarily capture all of these dimensions.

7. The organizational forms introduced in this chapter should be interpreted as developmental possibilities rather than fixed categories. Continued learning can increase integration, produce specialization, strengthen external dependence, internalize formerly external functions, or move previously internal operations into external tools and workflows. The important scientific question is therefore not only which organization a system presently exhibits, but which transitions remain available from that organization.

8. The "landscape of branching cognitive forms" is a prospective framework proposed in this book, not a prediction that future artificial intelligence must develop along specific predetermined paths. It emphasizes the possibility that increasingly capable systems may differ in integration, specialization, external dependence, self-correction, transfer, and developmental flexibility, producing several organizational forms rather than converging on a single endpoint.

CHAPTER 20

Understanding What We Built

Artificial intelligence entered history as an engineering achievement.

Its earliest defining questions were practical. Could a machine recognize a pattern, translate a sentence, classify an image, play a game, write code, or solve a problem? Progress meant making the system more accurate, efficient, flexible, and capable. Each advance widened the range of tasks that computation could perform.

That era has not ended.

Architectures will continue to improve. Training will become more efficient. Models will gain capabilities, tools, memory, and access to increasingly complex environments. Engineering will remain the force that creates new systems and expands what they can accomplish.

But engineering success has produced a second historical task.

Learning has created internal organizations that cannot be understood fully from their construction. The systems now contain representations, strategies, dependencies, competing processes, compensatory arrangements, and developmental trajectories that were not specified one by one. Their behavior can be measured, but measurement alone cannot explain what learning has made.

Artificial intelligence has therefore crossed a threshold.

The central problem is no longer only whether intelligent behavior can be produced.

It is how intelligence produced through learning should be understood.

20.1 When Building Creates a New Science

Useful technologies are often built before the principles governing them become clear.

The steam engine existed before thermodynamics provided a general account of heat, energy, and work. Engineering discovered how to construct machines that performed valuable functions. Science later explained why those machines behaved as they did, which principles extended beyond individual designs, and what those principles predicted about systems not yet built.

Artificial intelligence presents a comparable historical sequence, but with an unusual object.

The machinery was deliberately designed. The organization that emerged within it was learned.

Architectures, objectives, datasets, and optimization procedures established the conditions under which development occurred. They did not specify every concept, strategy, association, or computational route that later appeared. Training transformed a designed system into an empirical object whose mature organization required investigation.[1]

The transition from building to understanding does not mark the failure of engineering.

It marks the depth of its success.

A technology simple enough to remain completely transparent may never require a distinct science of its internal organization. Learned intelligence does. Its capabilities arise from distributed processes, interactions among mechanisms, accumulated history, and adaptation under changing conditions. The more powerful such systems become, the less adequate a purely construction-based account becomes.

The scientific questions now emerge from the achievements of engineering itself.

What organization did learning produce?

Why did that organization develop rather than another?

Which mechanisms support the system's present abilities?

How do those mechanisms interact, compete, compensate, and change?

What kinds of failure arise from the organization's strengths?

Which conclusions remain valid after continued learning or intervention?

What broader principles recur across independently developed systems?

These questions do not ask how to build intelligence again.

They ask what building intelligence has brought into existence.

20.2 What Progress Means Now

The meaning of progress changes once a technology becomes a scientific object.

Greater capability remains progress.

So do improved efficiency, broader transfer, stronger reasoning, and more reliable performance.

But another form of progress becomes possible.

A system is better understood when its internal observations can be connected into causal explanations. Understanding deepens when those explanations distinguish among competing mechanisms, predict what should happen under changing conditions, survive intervention, and remain accountable to later evidence.

Progress can therefore occur even when a model's benchmark score does not change.[2]

Discovering that a reliable capability depends on a fragile shortcut is progress.

Identifying that an intervention suppresses a behavior without repairing its mechanism is progress.

Learning that a model's effective intelligence depends on coordination with memory, tools, and verification processes is progress.

Determining that a conclusion applies only to one architecture or training history is also progress, because scientific knowledge becomes stronger when its boundaries are known.

This changes the questions asked of advanced systems.

A correct output is no longer the final unit of success.

A corrected behavior is no longer sufficient evidence of repair.

A powerful capability is no longer assumed to identify one kind of intelligence.

A stable performance pattern is no longer taken as proof of an unchanged mechanism.

Each result becomes the beginning of a more demanding inquiry into the organization beneath it.

This does not make performance less important.

It makes performance scientifically informative.

Behavior becomes evidence about a system whose internal condition must be reconstructed rather than assumed. Intervention becomes evidence about what can change, what remains, and which dependencies preserve function. Continued learning becomes evidence about the paths through which cognitive organization develops.

The field advances not only by producing better systems, but by increasing the precision of the explanations attached to them.

That change may ultimately alter how AI research describes its own achievements.

A model may be called more capable because it performs more tasks.

It may be called better understood because researchers can explain which organization supports those tasks, how that organization emerged, where it remains fragile, and how it is likely to respond when conditions change.

Capability and understanding can then progress together rather than being mistaken for the same accomplishment.

20.3 The Beginning of Artificial Cognitive Medicine

Artificial Cognitive Medicine gives this scientific task a coherent form.

It does not represent the end of inquiry into learned intelligence. It represents the beginning of a research program centered on a new class of engineered systems whose cognitive organization develops through learning.[3]

Artificial Cognitive Medicine begins with individual learned systems but does not end there. Its investigations can connect present condition, developmental change, intervention, and comparison across systems into an expanding account of learned intelligence.

That program will grow through discoveries that cannot yet be anticipated.

New methods may expose forms of internal organization that present techniques cannot resolve. Systems may develop new relationships with tools, memory, environments, and other models. Mechanisms now treated as unified may divide into several distinct processes. Apparently different findings may turn out to express one deeper organizational principle.

The discipline will therefore change as its object changes.

Its concepts will become more precise, its explanations more bounded, and its predictions more accountable to systems whose organization continues to change.

This openness is not a weakness. It is the condition of a developing science.[4]

A field becomes scientifically powerful not when every question has been settled, but when uncertainty can be organized into investigations that produce increasingly constrained explanations. Artificial Cognitive Medicine supplies that direction. It treats learned intelligence as something whose organization can be studied, whose condition can be explained, and whose development can continue teaching us what intelligence is capable of becoming.

The field will not develop through one decisive experiment.

It will grow through the accumulation of histories, interventions, comparisons, failed predictions, revised explanations, and recurring principles across generations of systems.

Each investigation will reveal only part of the landscape.

Together, they may create the first systematic science of intelligence developed inside machines.

20.4 Understanding What We Built

The paradox at the beginning of this book was simple.

We designed the machinery of learning before we understood the organization learning would produce.

That sequence once appeared to be a temporary gap. Better tools, larger datasets, or more detailed observation might eventually expose enough internal structure to close it.

The problem proved deeper.

Understanding learned intelligence requires more than opening a black box. It requires explanations capable of following organization through development, intervention, and change while remaining accountable to evidence across systems.

The mystery was never simply that the system contained hidden components.

It was that learning had created an organized intelligence whose meaning could not be read directly from either its code or its behavior.

That is why the solution could not be one interpretability method, one benchmark, one intervention, or one theory.

A new scientific attitude was required.

The trained system had to become evidence.

Its history had to become explanatory.

Its failures had to become symptoms rather than labels.

Its mechanisms had to be compared, tested, and followed through change.

Its improvement had to be distinguished from suppression and compensation.

Its differences from other systems had to become a source of general knowledge.

These changes redefine what it means to understand artificial intelligence.

Understanding is not possession of every parameter value.

It is not complete prediction of every output.

It is not a final map in which every component has been assigned one permanent function.

Understanding is an evidence-based account of how a learned organization developed, how it produces its present behavior, how it may change, and why the account should be revised when new evidence appears.[5]

That understanding will always remain incomplete.

But incompleteness does not make it arbitrary.

Scientific knowledge grows by narrowing what remains possible, identifying what the evidence supports, and building explanations strong enough to survive comparison with the systems themselves.

Artificial intelligence began by asking whether machines could behave intelligently.

Engineering answered that question more powerfully than earlier generations could have imagined.

The result created a harder question.

What kind of intelligence did learning produce inside the machines we built?

The answer will not come from capability alone.

It will emerge from histories reconstructed, mechanisms examined, explanations tested, trajectories followed, interventions evaluated, and principles compared across systems whose organization continues to develop.

We first learned to build machines capable of intelligent behavior.

We then learned to look inside them.

We are now beginning to investigate them as developing cognitive systems.

The next era of artificial intelligence will not be defined only by how much more capable those systems become.

It will also be defined by whether we learn to understand the intelligence we have already created.[6]

ENDNOTES

1. Modern machine-learning systems are engineered through architectures, objectives, datasets, optimization procedures, and computational infrastructure, while much of their detailed functional organization emerges through training rather than being specified component by component. Treating the resulting trained organization as an empirical object of investigation is a central premise of the framework developed in this book.

2. Scientific progress in the study of learned systems need not coincide with improvement in benchmark performance. Progress can also consist of identifying the mechanism underlying an existing capability, distinguishing robust generalization from shortcut dependence, determining whether an intervention produced repair or suppression, establishing the dependencies that preserve performance, or defining the conditions under which a mechanistic explanation remains valid.

3. *Artificial Cognitive Medicine* is the proposed scientific framework developed in this book. It organizes the investigation of learned artificial systems around developmental history, present organization, mechanistic explanation, diagnosis, prognosis, intervention, follow-up, and comparison across systems. The term is methodological rather than medical and does not imply that artificial systems are biological patients or subjects of literal clinical practice.

4. A developing scientific framework must remain revisable as new evidence, methods, and systems expose limitations in its existing concepts. Artificial Cognitive Medicine is therefore presented as a research program whose categories, distinctions, and explanatory principles should become more precise, divide, merge, or be abandoned when evidence requires revision.

5. The definition of understanding offered here is the book's proposed scientific standard for learned artificial systems. It does not require exhaustive knowledge of every parameter or perfect prediction of every possible output. It requires an evidence-based explanation connecting developmental history, present organization, causal mechanism, behavior, response to intervention, future change, and revision in light of subsequent evidence.

6. The concluding claim is prospective rather than predictive. The framework does not assume that future artificial-intelligence research will adopt Artificial Cognitive Medicine as presented here. It proposes that as learned systems become more capable and organizationally complex, scientific progress will increasingly depend on explaining what learning has produced rather than measuring capability alone.

Author's Note

A scientific idea begins differently from a scientific field.

An idea can be stated by one person. A field emerges only when many investigators begin asking questions that connect, when concepts become precise enough to test, when methods expose weaknesses in existing explanations, and when evidence determines which parts of an idea survive.

Artificial Cognitive Medicine begins here as such an idea.

The concepts proposed in these pages become scientifically meaningful when they generate discriminating questions, testable predictions, causal interventions, and explanations that remain accountable to later evidence.

As investigations accumulate, new forms of learned intelligence may require concepts that do not yet exist. New methods may reveal internal organizations that current techniques cannot detect, while comparisons across systems may show that apparently general mechanisms belong only to particular architectures, training histories, or environments.

That is how scientific ideas develop.

Their strength does not come from remaining unchanged. It comes from becoming more precise under pressure from evidence.

The same principle applies to Artificial Cognitive Medicine. Its development would require researchers to determine which concepts produce useful experiments, which distinctions improve explanation, which predictions survive testing, and which claims need to be narrowed, revised, or abandoned. Findings from individual systems would need to become comparable across models, architectures, developmental histories, and changing forms of artificial intelligence.

The result may not look exactly like the framework presented here.

It should not have to.

A productive scientific framework creates the conditions for its own refinement. It gives investigators a way to formulate problems clearly enough that evidence can change the framework itself. Concepts become more precise. Boundaries move. Categories divide or merge. Explanations that once seemed sufficient give way to stronger ones.

What matters is whether the underlying questions continue to generate knowledge.

The underlying scientific problems will become increasingly important as artificial intelligence develops beyond the systems that exist today. Future models may acquire longer memories, greater autonomy, richer interactions with tools and environments, new forms of adaptation, and internal organizations unlike those currently available for study. The scientific language used to investigate them will have to develop alongside them.

What that language becomes will ultimately be determined through scientific use.

Observation will reveal possibilities. Comparison will show which findings recur. Intervention will test causal claims. Prediction will expose explanations to conditions that have not yet occurred. Replication will determine how far a result can travel. Revision will keep the science responsive when new evidence changes what can reasonably be concluded.

What survives will do so because evidence continues to support it. What fails will make room for something better.

Artificial Cognitive Medicine should develop in the same way.

Its future begins not with preserving the framework exactly as it stands, but with putting it to work.

Glossary

Artificial Cognitive Medicine
A proposed scientific discipline for investigating the development, present organization, mechanisms, condition, future trajectories, and responses to intervention of learned artificial systems through examination, mechanistic explanation, diagnosis, prognosis, intervention, and follow-up.

Artificial Patient
A particular learned artificial system approached as the individual object of a structured scientific investigation through its developmental history, present organization, observable behavior, internal mechanisms, future trajectories, and responses to intervention.

Behavioral recovery
The disappearance or reduction of an unwanted response and improvement in observable performance under the tested conditions, whether or not the underlying mechanism has been repaired.

Compensation
The preservation or recovery of performance through an alternative or corrective process while the original weakness, limitation, or disrupted mechanism remains unresolved.

Compensatory recovery
Improvement produced by an alternative or corrective mechanism that preserves performance even though the original problematic process remains active or unresolved.

Computation
The process through which represented information is selected, transformed, combined, and used to produce an outcome.

Degeneracy
The capacity of structurally or computationally different mechanisms to support similar functions or produce comparable outcomes. Unlike redundancy, degeneracy does not require duplicate components performing essentially the same operation.

Developmental history
The accumulated sequence of initial conditions, training, later tuning, feedback, deployment, and continued adaptation through which a learned system acquired its present organization.

Diagnosis
The mechanism or mechanistic account most consistent with the available evidence in a particular learned system under defined conditions.

Differential diagnosis
The structured comparison of competing mechanistic explanations for an observed symptom, using their differing predictions to determine which account best fits the evidence.

Examination
The systematic investigation of a learned system's present condition, including what it represents, which internal processes become active, how information moves, which components contribute causally, and whether the observed organization remains stable across conditions.

Examination profile
An integrated account of how a learned system is organized during the computation under investigation, based on evidence about representations, activity, pathways, causal contributions, competing processes, and stability across conditions.

Follow-up
The continued investigation of a system after diagnosis or intervention to determine what changed, whether the original explanation remains valid, and how the system's organization develops over time.

Internal organization
The arrangement and interaction of representations, pathways, computational processes, competing mechanisms, and stabilizing relationships within a learned system.

Intervention
A deliberate alteration of an internal component, pathway, representation, learning condition, or surrounding condition used to test causal claims or change the system's organization.

Mechanism
An internal process or organized interaction among components that contributes causally to a behavior, capability, failure, or change.

Mechanistic explanation
An evidence-based account of how internal representations, components, pathways, and interactions produce a particular behavior, capability, failure, or change.

Mechanistic interpretability
The investigation of how internal representations, components, activations, and computational pathways contribute to a model's computations and behavior.

Mechanistic recovery
A change in which the underlying process responsible for a failure is repaired, weakened, reorganized, or replaced so that the improved behavior arises from a corrected internal organization.

Perturbation
A controlled experimental alteration of internal activity, a component, or a pathway used to test its causal contribution to a computation or behavior.

Prognosis
An evidence-based account of how a system's organization, mechanisms, or behavior is likely to persist or change under defined future conditions.

Redundancy
The presence of duplicate or closely equivalent components capable of performing substantially the same operation. Redundancy differs from degeneracy, in which structurally or computationally different mechanisms produce comparable outcomes.

Representation
An internal pattern or configuration through which a learned system encodes information, features, concepts, distinctions, or relationships.

Symptom
An observable behavioral manifestation whose underlying mechanism has not yet been established. A symptom records what occurred without identifying the internal condition that produced it.

Symptom suppression
The prevention or concealment of an unwanted outward response while the internal mechanism responsible for the original failure remains substantially intact.

Trajectory
The path through which a system's organization, mechanisms, or behavior persists, develops, or reorganizes over time and under changing conditions.

Working diagnosis
The mechanistic explanation that currently organizes the evidence better than its alternatives, while remaining provisional and open to revision as new evidence appears.

Selected References and Further Reading

Artificial Cognitive Medicine draws on several established intellectual and scientific traditions, including artificial intelligence, mechanistic interpretability, neuroscience, complex-systems research, causal reasoning, scientific explanation, learning theory, and clinical reasoning. The works below offer selected pathways into the foundational ideas, methods, and research questions developed throughout this book.

Foundations of Artificial Intelligence and Deep Learning

Books

Bishop, Christopher M. *Pattern Recognition and Machine Learning.* New York: Springer, 2006.

Goodfellow, Ian, Yoshua Bengio, and Aaron Courville. *Deep Learning.* Cambridge, MA: MIT Press, 2016.

Murphy, Kevin P. *Probabilistic Machine Learning: An Introduction.* Cambridge, MA: MIT Press, 2022.

Prince, Simon J. D. *Understanding Deep Learning.* Cambridge, MA: MIT Press, 2023.

Research Articles

Bengio, Yoshua, Aaron Courville, and Pascal Vincent. "Representation Learning: A Review and New Perspectives." *IEEE Transactions on Pattern Analysis and Machine Intelligence* 35, no. 8 (2013): 1798–1828.

Brown, Tom B., Benjamin Mann, Nick Ryder, Melanie Subbiah, Jared Kaplan, Prafulla Dhariwal, et al. "Language Models Are Few-Shot Learners." In *Advances in Neural Information Processing Systems* 33 (2020): 1877–1901.

LeCun, Yann, Yoshua Bengio, and Geoffrey Hinton. "Deep Learning." *Nature* 521 (2015): 436–444.

Rumelhart, David E., Geoffrey E. Hinton, and Ronald J. Williams. "Learning Representations by Back-Propagating Errors." *Nature* 323 (1986): 533–536.

Vaswani, Ashish, Noam Shazeer, Niki Parmar, Jakob Uszkoreit, Llion Jones, Aidan N. Gomez, et al. "Attention Is All You Need." In *Advances in Neural Information Processing Systems* 30 (2017): 5998–6008.

Mechanistic Interpretability

Bau, David, Bolei Zhou, Aditya Khosla, Aude Oliva, and Antonio Torralba. "Network Dissection: Quantifying Interpretability of Deep Visual Representations." In *Proceedings of the IEEE Conference on Computer Vision and Pattern Recognition* (2017): 6541–6549.

Belinkov, Yonatan. "Probing Classifiers: Promises, Shortcomings, and Advances." *Computational Linguistics* 48, no. 1 (2022): 207–219.

Conmy, Arthur, Augustine N. Mavor-Parker, Aengus Lynch, Stefan Heimersheim, and Adrià Garriga-Alonso. "Towards Automated Circuit Discovery for Mechanistic Interpretability." In *Advances in Neural Information Processing Systems* 36 (2023).

Elhage, Nelson, Tristan Hume, Catherine Olsson, Nicholas Schiefer, Tom Henighan, Shauna Kravec, et al. "Toy Models of Superposition." *arXiv* preprint arXiv:2209.10652 (2022).

Geiger, Atticus, Hanson Lu, Thomas Icard, and Christopher Potts. "Causal Abstractions of Neural Networks." In *Advances in Neural Information Processing Systems* 34 (2021): 9574–9586.

Huben, Robert, Hoagy Cunningham, Logan Smith, Aidan Ewart, and Lee Sharkey. "Sparse Autoencoders Find Highly Interpretable Features in Language Models." In *International Conference on Learning Representations* (2024).

Lipton, Zachary C. "The Mythos of Model Interpretability." *Communications of the ACM* 61, no. 10 (2018): 36–43.

Meng, Kevin, David Bau, Alex Andonian, and Yonatan Belinkov. "Locating and Editing Factual Associations in GPT." In *Advances in Neural Information Processing Systems* 35 (2022): 17359–17372.

Olah, Chris, Nick Cammarata, Ludwig Schubert, Gabriel Goh, Michael Petrov, and Shan Carter. "Zoom In: An Introduction to Circuits." *Distill* 5, no. 3 (2020). https://doi.org/10.23915/distill.00024.001.

Olsson, Catherine, Nelson Elhage, Neel Nanda, Nicholas Joseph, Nova DasSarma, Tom Henighan, et al. "In-context Learning and Induction Heads." *arXiv* preprint arXiv:2209.11895 (2022).

Wang, Kevin, Alexandre Variengien, Arthur Conmy, Buck Shlegeris, and Jacob Steinhardt. "Interpretability in the Wild: A Circuit for Indirect Object Identification in GPT-2 Small." In *International Conference on Learning Representations* (2023).

Neuroscience and Organized Cognition

Books

Kandel, Eric R., John D. Koester, Sarah H. Mack, and Steven A. Siegelbaum, eds. *Principles of Neural Science*. 6th ed. New York: McGraw Hill, 2021.

Sporns, Olaf. *Networks of the Brain*. Cambridge, MA: MIT Press, 2010.

Research Articles

Bassett, Danielle S., and Olaf Sporns. "Network Neuroscience." *Nature Neuroscience* 20, no. 3 (2017): 353–364.

Breakspear, Michael. "Dynamic Models of Large-Scale Brain Activity." *Nature Neuroscience* 20, no. 3 (2017): 340–352.

Draganski, Bogdan, Christian Gaser, Volker Busch, Gerhard Schuierer, Ulrich Bogdahn, and Arne May. "Neuroplasticity: Changes in Grey Matter Induced by Training." *Nature* 427, no. 6972 (2004): 311–312.

Edelman, Gerald M., and Joseph A. Gally. "Degeneracy and Complexity in Biological Systems." *Proceedings of the National Academy of Sciences of the United States of America* 98, no. 24 (2001): 13763–13768.

Nudo, Randolph J., Brenda M. Wise, F. SiFuentes, and Garrett W. Milliken. "Neural Substrates for the Effects of Rehabilitative Training on Motor Recovery after Ischemic Infarct." *Science* 272, no. 5269 (1996): 1791–1794.

Olshausen, Bruno A., and David J. Field. "Emergence of Simple-Cell Receptive Field Properties by Learning a Sparse Code for Natural Images." *Nature* 381 (1996): 607–609.

Ross, Lauren N., and Danielle S. Bassett. "Causation in Neuroscience: Keeping Mechanism Meaningful." *Nature Reviews Neuroscience* 25, no. 2 (2024): 81–90.

Seguin, Caio, Olaf Sporns, and Andrew Zalesky. "Brain Network Communication: Concepts, Models and Applications." *Nature Reviews Neuroscience* 24, no. 9 (2023): 557–574.

Silvanto, Juha, Zaira Cattaneo, Lorella Battelli, and Alvaro Pascual-Leone. "Baseline Cortical Excitability Determines Whether TMS Disrupts or Facilitates Behavior." *Journal of Neurophysiology* 99, no. 5 (2008): 2725–2730.

Learning, Development, and Continual Change

Books

Hebb, Donald O. *The Organization of Behavior*. New York: Wiley, 1949.

Rumelhart, David E., James L. McClelland, and the PDP Research Group. *Parallel Distributed Processing: Explorations in the Microstructure of Cognition*. 2 vols. Cambridge, MA: MIT Press, 1986.

Research Articles

Kirkpatrick, James, Razvan Pascanu, Neil Rabinowitz, Joel Veness, Guillaume Desjardins, Andrei A. Rusu, et al. "Overcoming Catastrophic Forgetting in Neural Networks." *Proceedings of the National Academy of Sciences* 114, no. 13 (2017): 3521–3526.

Parisi, German I., Ronald Kemker, Jose L. Part, Christopher Kanan, and Stefan Wermter. "Continual Lifelong Learning with Neural Networks: A Review." *Neural Networks* 113 (2019): 54–71.

Saxe, Andrew M., James L. McClelland, and Surya Ganguli. "A Mathematical Theory of Semantic Development in Deep Neural Networks." *Proceedings of the National Academy of Sciences* 116, no. 23 (2019): 11537–11546.

Complex Systems and Network Dynamics

Holland, John H. *Hidden Order: How Adaptation Builds Complexity*. Reading, MA: Addison-Wesley, 1995.

Mitchell, Melanie. *Complexity: A Guided Tour*. Oxford: Oxford University Press, 2009.

Strogatz, Steven H. *Nonlinear Dynamics and Chaos*. 2nd ed. Boulder, CO: Westview Press, 2015.

Causation, Mechanism, and Scientific Explanation

Craver, Carl F. *Explaining the Brain: Mechanisms and the Mosaic Unity of Neuroscience*. Oxford: Oxford University Press, 2007.

Lipton, Peter. *Inference to the Best Explanation*. 2nd ed. London: Routledge, 2004.

Pearl, Judea. *Causality: Models, Reasoning, and Inference*. 2nd ed. Cambridge: Cambridge University Press, 2009.

Woodward, James. *Making Things Happen: A Theory of Causal Explanation*. Oxford: Oxford University Press, 2003.

Diagnosis and Clinical Reasoning

Books

Kassirer, Jerome P., John B. Wong, and Richard I. Kopelman. *Learning Clinical Reasoning*. 2nd ed. Philadelphia: Lippincott Williams & Wilkins, 2010.

Simel, David L., and Drummond Rennie, eds. *The Rational Clinical Examination: Evidence-Based Clinical Diagnosis*. New York: McGraw Hill, 2009.

Research Articles

Croskerry, Pat. "The Importance of Cognitive Errors in Diagnosis and Strategies to Minimize Them." *Academic Medicine* 78, no. 8 (2003): 775–780.

Elstein, Arthur S., and Alan Schwarz. "Clinical Problem Solving and Diagnostic Decision Making: Selective Review of the Cognitive Literature." *BMJ* 324, no. 7339 (2002): 729–732.

Prediction, Intervention, Generalization, and Reproducibility

Books

Hernán, Miguel A., and James M. Robins. *Causal Inference: What If*. Boca Raton, FL: Chapman & Hall/CRC, 2020.

Research Articles

Hendrycks, Dan, and Thomas Dietterich. "Benchmarking Neural Network Robustness to Common Corruptions and Perturbations." In *Proceedings of the International Conference on Learning Representations* (2019).

Munafò, Marcus R., Brian A. Nosek, Dorothy V. M. Bishop, Katherine S. Button, Christopher D. Chambers, Nathalie Percie du Sert, et al. "A Manifesto for Reproducible Science." *Nature Human Behaviour* 1 (2017): 0021.

Nakkiran, Preetum, Gal Kaplun, Yamini Bansal, Tristan Yang, Boaz Barak, and Ilya Sutskever. "Deep Double Descent: Where Bigger Models and More Data Hurt." In *Proceedings of the International Conference on Learning Representations* (2020).

Shmueli, Galit. "To Explain or to Predict?" *Statistical Science* 25, no. 3 (2010): 289–310.

Yarkoni, Tal. "The Generalizability Crisis." *Behavioral and Brain Sciences* 45 (2022): e1.

About the Author

Moawiah Naffaa, PhD, is a neuroscientist and author whose work explores the intersection of neuroscience, artificial intelligence, cognition, and complex adaptive systems. His research has focused on neural development, stem cell biology, glial biology, neural plasticity, electrophysiology, and the mechanisms that shape brain function and disease.

Alongside his scientific publications, he has written a series of books examining intelligence, creativity, memory, meaning, and the evolving relationship between human and artificial cognition. His books include *Mind Engineered, Creativity Engineered, Echoes of the Pattern, Cognitive Saturation Shock*, and *Meaning by Design*. Together with his broader work in neuroscience, these explorations gradually led to the questions developed in this book.

In *The Mysterious Future of AI,* Naffaa proposes a framework for studying learned artificial systems through principles of scientific investigation informed by neuroscience and the study of complex adaptive systems. The book introduces the **Artificial Patient** and **Artificial Cognitive Medicine** as frameworks for investigating how artificial intelligence develops, how its internal organization produces behavior, how competing mechanistic explanations can be evaluated, how future trajectories may be predicted, and how systems change in response to intervention over time

www.ingramcontent.com/pod-product-compliance
Lightning Source LLC
LaVergne TN
LVHW010716061126
851857LV00014B/1216
* 9 7 9 8 2 5 6 2 8 1 0 9 0 *